learn work lead

Things Your Mentor Won't Tell You

TERRI TIERNEY CLARK

Praise for *Learn, Work, Lead: Things Your Mentor Won't Tell You*

"*Learn Work Lead* wakes you up and makes you focus on what to ask for and how to ask for it, rather than waiting for opportunities that may never occur."

—Sam Zell, Chairman,
Equity Group Investments

"No matter where you are in your career—starting out or fearlessly advancing to your next stage—there's something in this book that can help you get there a little faster."

—Kathryn Minshew,
Founder and CEO, TheMuse.com

"Terri has gathered a treasure trove of stories, experiences, wisdom, and insights to light the way in navigating your professional path. Her book is more than a 'how to' manual in that it's chock full of tools to help young women analyze and assess situations to make good decisions on their journey. I wish I'd had access to a book like *Learn, Work, Lead* as a resource early in my career and am grateful that my young granddaughter Teagan will."

—Jim Weber, CEO,
Brooks Running Company

"Terri's extraordinary experience in the male-dominated world of finance acts as a terrific foundation for preparing women to 'peel back and examine the layers of each situation' one faces throughout their career journey. Terri's tremendous insight enables young professional women to gain an understanding of the fundamental elements of leadership and to develop self-awareness, which is critical to future career success. Thank you, Terri, for creating such a practical and transformational resource for today's women. Your timing is perfect!"

—Herb Greenberg, Ph.D.,
CEO & Founder, Caliper

"*Learn, Work, Lead* is an incredibly practical guide to navigating the obstacles at work and making the most of your professional talents. This book is bursting with great advice."

—Linda Babcock, author
Ask For It: How Women Can Use the Power of Negotiation to Get What They Really Want

learn work lead

Things Your Mentor Won't Tell You

Learn, Work, Lead: Things Your Mentor Won't Tell You

Photo Credit: Eric Laurits

For more information, contact Peterson's, 3 Columbia Circle, Suite 205, Albany, NY 12203; 800-338-3282 Ext. 54229; or find us online at www.petersonsbooks.com.

ISBN: 978-0-7689-3893-7

Printed in the United States of America

10 9 8 7 6 5 4 3 2 1 16 15 14

First Edition

Dedication

To my parents, John and Stu, my original mentors,
and my family, Jon, Devon, Hunter, and Jack,
always my inspiration.

Table of Contents

Foreword

"Where do you see yourself in ten years?" It's a classic interview question many of us have faced.

For those just starting out in their careers, the answer can be fraught with anxiety. Developing strong personal relationships, understanding how others see you in the workplace, and becoming indispensable (and promotable!)—these are all critical skills and lessons that can feel overwhelming at times. While countless people are asking themselves, "What do I want to do with my life (and how am I going to get there)?" few have had the guidance, mentorship, and advice needed to turn those dreams into reality. Reading *Learn, Work, Lead* can be your first step.

Professional women today are entering an unprecedented era of flexibility and mobility. But to take advantage of the career opportunities available to you, it helps to develop the right skills and frameworks for making informed choices along the way. Success in the workplace is often a series of small steps, phrasings, and statements: the way influence and authority are communicated subtly or the dance of negotiation between an individual and her boss. Together, these nuances form the unwritten rules that help the workplace function—and decide who gets ahead.

Many have the impression that these skills are innate, something a few lucky individuals are born with, but for most of us, that couldn't be further from the truth. Many successful leaders weren't genetically gifted with business acumen at the start of their careers; rather, they learned from career setbacks that taught them to approach their careers more analytically and develop their own *True North* from the advice that they had been given.

In the following pages, Terri Tierney Clark will help you navigate your career to become an invaluable team member, assert yourself in the office, build strong professional relationships, and gain professional respect within your organization. She will teach you how to assess your career, every step of the way, to get you where you want to go.

If you're reading this book, it means you're passionate about your career, and I couldn't be more excited by what the future has in store for you. I believe that you can and should love your job, and that successfully navigating your career requires a bit of advice, direction, and some tough love. Now more than ever before, you have the opportunity to find a career that inspires you—and thrive in it—but you must take advantage of the tools available to you.

No matter where you are in your career—starting out or fearlessly advancing to your next stage—there's something in this book that can help you get there a little faster. Be curious, stay passionate, and learn from those around you. And most importantly, use your knowledge to *develop your own voice*—the world is listening.

—Kathryn Minshew
Founder and CEO
TheMuse.com

Introduction

It is better to look ahead and prepare than to look back and regret.

—Jackie Joyner-Kersee, Olympic Gold Medalist

Imagine you're a female reporter in an NFL locker room after a game. Testosterone-inspired voices are shouting, making it hard for you to be heard above the noise. Men walk past you, oblivious that their words and actions may make you uncomfortable. As the only woman in the room, you try to strike that perfect balance of being confident, but not pushy, knowledgeable, but not arrogant, and authoritative, but not masculine. You keep thinking there should be a playbook for all this stuff! That's how it felt to be a female managing director on Wall Street in the 1990s. And like the first female reporters allowed in the locker rooms, we didn't have other women around who could show us the ropes. Mentoring by men or women hadn't yet come into vogue so most of us didn't even have career advisors; we just made it up as we went along. Fortunately, businesses have progressed and professional women today have far more opportunities to get the guidance they need. They have mentors, female executives to call on, and plenty of career resources available to them.

But sometimes today's professional women act on career advice without giving enough thought to the advice that they are given. They accept their mentors' suggestions as the final word when the advice might not be right for them. Mentors can't possibly understand all of their protégés' motivations. The mentors' own experiences may also excessively influence their views. And, as I pointed out to a young woman recently, "There are things your mentor won't tell you. You'll have to figure them out for yourself."

Some women know how to weigh the advice they're given but don't always know what direction to take when career plans don't work out. A recent graduate told me she couldn't figure out why she hadn't received any offers for full-time jobs. The summer before, every recruiter she met had called her back for second interviews. By the end of her search she had three offers. But now the recruiters weren't interested, and she didn't know why. After I heard her story I realized she was excluding some information during her interviews that was costing her the callbacks. She hadn't realized her mistake because she hadn't acquired the necessary tools to solve tough job-search and career dilemmas.

This woman, like many others, needs to learn how to attack career problems to uncover the right solutions. When I attended business school we analyzed case studies as if we were **peeling an onion,** looking at all the possible outcomes of different decisions. *Learn, Work, Lead* will show you how to peel back and examine the layers of each situation before you decide which direction to take. The career case stories presented throughout this book will teach you how to think through problems and solutions so that you can take the same approach with your own career.

I wrote *Learn, Work, Lead* to help women professionals learn how to analyze career decisions and make the best choices. After reading this book you will be able to evaluate all of the information available to you from your mentors and others to determine the right path. You will know how to plan for your optimal career and to succeed, even when you're faced with problems that no one could predict.

You will become an expert at peeling the onion.

Chapter 1: The New Careerist

My dear, here we must run as fast as we can, just to stay in place. And if you wish to go anywhere you must run twice as fast as that.

—The Queen of Hearts, *Alice in Wonderland*

It was 10 p.m., and I was at the office staring at a spreadsheet that hadn't changed for an hour. I checked my numbers over and over but still couldn't find the problem. So I trashed the original work and built a new model. After a while I realized that my spreadsheet looked identical to the first one, including the same error. The work was due in the morning, and I had no idea how to proceed. At this point I'm pretty sure I prayed—possibly promising to forgo chocolate and the rest of my vices if my prayers were answered. I really needed a miracle right about then.

At the time of this career trauma I had been working on Wall Street for just a few weeks. Work had gone smoothly, probably because there was always someone around when I needed to ask questions. My mistake that day was putting off the assignment. The project looked similar to one I had just finished so I didn't think it would be difficult. A friend was in from out of town, and I decided to meet her for dinner and start the assignment when I returned. Initially things went smoothly. Then I noticed the error and dug in to try and fix it. Whatever number crunching I tried didn't work. I looked around. Everyone was gone by this point. And there was no point in calling anyone; this wasn't the kind of thing that anyone could help me with over the phone. An hour passed, and I wasn't any closer to figuring out how to find the error. Then I heard someone's voice.

"Hey, have any food around here?" asked Matt, a friendly second-year analyst from the Mergers and Acquisitions Department. He was scavenging for take-out while his printing job finished. I must have looked desperate because he asked if I was OK.

"Yes, oh yes . . . . Thank God you're here, can you help me?" I answered. Matt took about five minutes to figure out my problem and then stayed to help me finish the spreadsheet. I repaid him as best I could with a bag of chips from a nearby desk.

What I thought of as a near-death experience at the time taught me a lesson about priorities. Most ***New Careerists*** *will have similar experiences that create "aha!" moments for them as well. But trial and error is what the first stage of your career is all about. And if you're prepared, you're likely to learn gracefully without too many heart-racing episodes like the one I had.*

The New Careerist stage can last from three to eight years. How long each professional stays in that stage depends on the industry, the company, and of course the person. The number of years of education you have could influence the amount of time you will need to spend in the first stage as well. Employees with advanced degrees might move faster up the ranks, although in some organizations the benefit of their degrees won't kick in until later. And if you work a few years, go back to school for graduate work and return to the workforce, you may still be in stage one for a while, even though your advanced degree will likely open up options for you down the road.

Make Your Boss Look Good

As a new employee, producing accurate and timely work will impress your boss and make him look good to his superiors and clients. And your boss understands that he's only as good as the team supporting him, so his success reflects well upon you. As you complete your projects, always take a step back and think about the end use and how your manager will use the information. Is it for a client pitch or an internal memo? How can you prepare the material to conform to his request but also make it easy for him to use for the specific purpose? If you take into account your boss's needs, he will consider you a more valuable employee.

Accuracy and Dependability

Your manager relies on you to deliver accurate work. Anything less will waste his time but could have worse consequences. Your mistakes could embarrass him in front of clients and colleagues or lose business for your company. And it's important to realize that work is not like school where one mistake on a test might give you a 94%. There's no partial credit in the office, so an error at work could earn you an F.

The stakes are high on the job because one error can throw off an entire business analysis. The analysis gets further skewed if you're tasked with going back and showing various permutations of the work you developed. You begin to create a totally fictitious picture because all of the changes hinge on the one error you made. Depending on your manager and the importance of the project you're working on, you may or may not get your head handed to you. Hopefully your boss sees the mistake as a learning experience because, well, everyone makes mistakes. But if you are one of those workers who consistently makes errors, your manager will stop trusting you with key projects. So please take the time to check and double-check your work.

In addition to your own, you may need to check others' work too. If you are given an assignment with another junior colleague, the two of you should make sure it's perfect before handing it over to your boss. Even if your colleague made the mistake, you'll both likely be blamed. And this advice doesn't just apply to number crunching. I once asked my assistant to make a lunch reservation for a prospective client meeting, but she forgot. When we arrived at the restaurant the hostess told us we had no reservation and would have to wait 15 minutes for our table. My boss glared at me with a *wait till I get you home* look that made me feel like I was 12 years old. That incident made me realize that a mistake like that was not my assistant's fault but mine. I should have confirmed the reservation with her.

In addition to checking your work, make sure you can defend it. If you used sources to complete your project, whether they were company documents or advice from senior professionals, make sure you have those sources available for reference. You should also be prepared to discuss the business assumptions that you made to complete your work. If you take steps to show your superiors that your work is defensible, you're likely to receive more significant projects in the future.

Sometimes professionals make errors because they don't carry out their manager's instructions. When your boss discusses a project with you, listen closely and ask questions to make sure you understand exactly what he wants. If you have additional questions later, gather them up and ask them at one time so you don't interrupt him too often. Your manager wants to view you as an independent operator who can get the job done without needing assistance every 30 minutes. If you are fundamentally lacking the skills you need to do your basic work, get help from a peer. If your job requires competency with a program like Excel or JavaScript and you don't know it cold, you may be taking more time than your manager expects on a project. Take time between projects, at night or at home, practicing with the program until you get up to speed. And finally, if you have a suggestion for a change to the project, make sure you have cleared the change with your manager before you implement it.

Time Is of the Essence

Even if you produce perfect work, it isn't any use if you deliver it after it is needed. If it appears that the assignment will take longer than you anticipated, discuss the issue with your manager. She may be more concerned about the deadline than other aspects of the project and decide to shorten its scope. Or she may give you more time or some help to get it done by the original deadline. You can't understand her priorities unless you ask, so don't be afraid to approach her with your timing problem before it's too late. Also, make sure you know whether you have a timing problem in the first place. If your manager doesn't tell you when an assignment is due, either inquire or suggest a time when you believe you can complete it, and ask if that timing works. If she agrees, your suggested timing becomes your deadline and you need to push to finish it by then.

And project or not, it's a good idea to respond in a timely manner in the office—*especially* with senior executives. No one likes to be kept hanging, so if you don't have an answer right away, tell your co-worker that you will get back to her shortly. That's obvious advice in a face-to-face conversation, but many people don't realize that in an e-mail you should also respond as quickly as possible, even if it's just to let your colleague know you are tracking down the answer.

If you are sitting on the other side of the request queue, you may become frustrated when you don't receive a response. After a respectable amount of time you can request again. Just make sure you use a neutral tone, like "Hey, I'm just checking in to see if you gave some thought to my question." Sometimes, walking down the hall and requesting in person works a lot better when you are trying to get an answer.

From time to time, you may receive a *pocket veto,* an implicit *no* by non-response. There's not much you can do about that situation, and if you press you still won't get the answer you're looking for. But don't jump to any conclusions; the person may not answer you, either because of the time required or because the answer isn't what you want to hear, so she just doesn't respond at all. It doesn't mean she dislikes you or never wants to work with you; it just means she didn't answer you.

As a new professional, you will be on the waiting end of information gathering much of the time. It's often more convenient to e-mail requests for information, but (despite a recent generational aversion to talking on phones) sometimes you need to make a phone call. If a senior colleague asks for some material she requested and you respond, "I e-mailed a few days ago and haven't heard back," she will probably make it clear to you that you need to pick up the phone and call.

NOTE TO FILE: 

- Check your work. Rinse and repeat.
- Your manager may not say anything if you miss a deadline, but she noticed.

Find Your Voice

My husband, Jon Clark, also started his career on Wall Street. He remembers the incident that changed him from being what he calls an "order taker" to becoming a real contributor. He was on one of his first assignments and had produced a spreadsheet just as he had been directed. He checked it over and brought it into the banker who requested it.

"Thanks," Ned said as Jon handed over the work and waited for comments. "So what does this analysis tell me?" Ned asked Jon.

Jon stared at him a moment, then read off the numbers on the sheet, "It tells you income is x, and cash flow is y."

Ned handed Jon the spreadsheet. "Go back and figure out what these numbers mean. Then come tell me."

Ned was teaching Jon that his job was not only to crunch the numbers but to understand his analysis. Ned wanted Jon to be able to contribute to the discussion on the transaction. Oftentimes the junior employees who are closest to the work can pick out trends or abnormalities better than their more seasoned bosses. Ned wanted Jon to be that valuable type of employee. Quickly Jon learned not to just do the work, but to understand the work and understand the business.

As my husband discovered, work begins to get a lot more interesting as you gain comfort at your job and ***find your voice.*** *Finding your voice means having the confidence and conviction to offer supportable ideas to your team. Most new professionals gain this comfort level once they have completed a few projects and begin to feel that they have a relatively solid appreciation of the industry. They understand their group's objectives and the work becomes intuitive. When you begin to develop that comfort level, you want to go beyond what's asked of you and begin to contribute your insights as well.*

You also want to exceed expectations by taking your project to the next level or asking for additional work that will help build your skill base. Or you can lend your creativity to an issue that no one else has noticed or taken the time to address. All of these initiatives will help your manager begin to view you as someone capable of taking on the next tier of responsibility.

Assert Yourself

In a National Institutes of Health study[1] on negotiation, researchers found that women curtailed their assertiveness for fear it would be perceived negatively and cause a backlash. As a result, the women were less successful in negotiations. A separate study, by scholars at Princeton and Brigham Young universities, considered whether women speak as much as men in team situations. In the majority of the groups polled, women spoke less than 75 percent of the time that men spoke.

These results mean that the odds are against women who attempt to voice their views. Men have louder, booming voices and tend to interrupt[2] more than women. Even when women realize they are being inadvertently silenced in group settings, they often are unable to change the situation. The solution is practice. If you don't feel comfortable contributing when you think you should, start by offering your input in one-on-one or small group meetings with a receptive audience such as close co-workers. Rehearse your proposal, no matter how brief, and make yourself aware of counter-arguments, so that you come off sounding articulate and knowledgeable. And importantly, speak up. If you talk loudly and with confidence, amazingly, your ideas sound a lot better to others. If your suggestions are dismissed, that's OK too. Business is an exchange of creative ideas that results in decisions being made. You have plenty of time to advance other thoughts. Even if you are overruled, your manager will gain a higher opinion of you for showing initiative.

I had my ideas rejected plenty of times as a young professional, and it wasn't until later in my career that I could appreciate that my boss had good reasons to rebuff my work. My superiors' experience, client issues, and office politics all played a role in their decisions.

During the summer before my second year in business school, I worked in the Jell-O Pudding division of General Foods. My manager asked me to analyze figures for chocolate pudding sales in the Midwest vs. the Southeast. I completed the analysis by applying something I learned in my statistics class and determined that we should increase marketing efforts in the Midwest and cut back ad dollars in the Southeast. My boss took a long look at my regression analysis and then decided we were going to maintain the marketing plan as it was. He explained that he had managed the brand for years and had a feeling the current plan was appropriate. Subsequent sales figures showed that his assumption was correct.

So why did he have me analyze the numbers? His theory was that it's important to see what the analysis shows, but it shouldn't be the only factor in making business decisions. His experience in growth periods, market slowdowns, and prior advertising campaigns all entered into his judgment. Ultimately, he had to live with his decision and just had a sense based upon his accumulated knowledge that he should ignore the analysis.

Client priorities can also influence a manager's decision. When I was an associate at Merrill Lynch, my manager asked me to analyze whether we should undertake a certain transaction. The transaction was small, would break even at best, and possibly lose money for Merrill. So I suggested we pass. Once again my recommendation was nixed. My manager told me that we were trying to develop this particular client because future business would be much more significant.

Why didn't my boss tell me about the hidden agenda in the first place? I was new to the group so maybe he was trying to vet my analytical abilities. He also may have used the information to see just how unprofitable the transaction would be. Or possibly he didn't want to undertake the transaction altogether, which was forced on him from above, and he needed a record of our analysis in case questions arose later. There could have been a number of reasons he had me do the analysis.

Office politics is another possible explanation for your recommendations not being adopted. Your boss may believe that your group will benefit from what looks like an ill-advised decision because it will gain favorable attention from senior managers, regardless of the outcome. In those types of situations, your manager may not feel comfortable giving you a reason for turning you down.

As my career evolved I began to understand, and even make, some of these types of decisions that relied more on experience than analysis. Overall, experience trumps pure analysis in the business world. But don't let rejection hold you back from contributing. Establishing yourself as someone with a unique voice is a critical step towards advancing to the next stage of your career.

The Office Meeting

Hopefully your manager will invite you to meetings pertaining to your projects. If you have developed material for a meeting and haven't been invited, you should ask if you can go. She may be happy to have you there or may have reasons for excluding you, including the number of people already attending. One thing is for sure though, if you don't ask, you won't attend.

It wouldn't seem appropriate after reading Sheryl Sandberg's influential book *Lean In*[3] to refrain from advising you to, well, *lean in.* Sandberg references women at a meeting who sat in chairs off to the side of the room instead of around the conference table where the men sat. "I motioned for the women to come sit at the table," Sandberg writes, "waving them over so they would feel welcomed. They demurred and remained in their seats." Sandberg stresses that women need to sit at the table, to lean in and not fade back. Agreed, and not only should you lean in, you should speak up.

A friend of mine told me about her first interdepartment meeting at her post-college job. She was excited to be invited and made sure to be ready for questions from her manager. He didn't ask any, so she exhaled a bit walking out of the meeting. But he stopped her right away. "Lauren," he said, "you didn't say anything. Always say something; otherwise you're invisible to everyone there." Lauren didn't understand that to build her reputation at her company, she had to start developing her image right away. Because of her work, she knew parts of the discussion topic better than anyone. She could have cleared up some confusion but she didn't want to appear intrusive. Yet she would have been helpful, not intrusive, had she voiced her opinion. If you are in a similar situation and can't think of anything to add, ask a brilliant question instead. Sometimes, asking questions can make you look even smarter than making statements.

The only exception to the rule of **at least saying one thing** at a meeting is if you are a summer intern or brand-new hire. If you're either, there's a good chance you haven't spent enough time at your company to understand much of the discussion at the meeting. So relax—the pressure is off. You can listen and learn silently unless you know you can be additive.

NOTE TO FILE: 

- If you present an idea that's not adopted, don't take it personally. Smile and move on.

Be Promotable

Even if you make your boss look good and develop your voice within your organization, you won't necessarily be making yourself promotable to the next level. You will also need to demonstrate the maturity of a senior executive by developing your personal skills and projecting the right kind of attitude.

Polish Your Soft Skills

When I was 16, my mother told me that I had poise. *Poise* sounded tremendously uncool to me. I wanted to be hot, not have poise. I was pretty sure the two states were mutually exclusive. When I looked up "poise" in the dictionary, I read, "graceful and elegant bearing in a person." I knew I was doomed.

Thank goodness those years are over. I did come to appreciate my mother's portrayal of me, or more appropriately, her efforts to raise me to gain poise and self-assurance. I'm sure it helped me during my first job interviews and formed the base of personality skills that I continued to develop over the course of my career.

Poise, confidence, agreeableness, persuasiveness, as well as communication and language skills, form the cluster of abilities known as **Soft Skills.** These skills, which relate to how you present yourself to your colleagues and clients, will be the critical indicators of your success. It may seem counterintuitive that you need to spend time developing personal skills when you may be the hardest worker among your peers. But even though work product is critical, soft skills will become increasingly important as you rise in seniority. At the very top of organizations, executives achieve their spots at the helm more often as a direct result of their leadership style than of their raw intelligence, industry knowledge, and work ethic. A CEO usually rises to the top of an organization because of a track record of great successes. Those successes indicate the leader is adept at teamwork and forming coalitions to help push ideas through.

Polished soft skills are necessary not only for the leaders of your organization but for professionals in all stages of their careers. Often when managers talk about **fitting in** with the team, they are referring to the ability of a worker to relate to her team members and be able to discuss alternate views in a professional and tactful way. This ability is part of displaying effective soft skills. Some people are born with these skills. Some cultivated them from family members who set good examples. Fortunately, those who weren't blessed by fate can still raise their social IQ by acquiring these necessary skills. You can study the style of business people you respect, then practice adopting their skills. Or, you can take courses, at work or outside, that teach leadership training.

Attitude

Your manager wants to believe you like her and enjoy your job, or at least that you won't spit in her coffee when she looks away. At the office, attitude counts for a lot. That means, no matter how miserable you are, you need to look happy. If you're feeling frustrated, most of the time it's not the work, it's the work-giver. Difficult superiors are an occupational hazard in any office. To make your life easier, you need to separate the work from the person doling out the work. You can then more easily adjust your attitude, so the rest of the department doesn't catch on.

I noticed a blog exchange on attitude recently on a great go-to website for aspiring financial professionals. The website, *Wall Street Oasis,*[4] is written by Wall Streeters for Wall Streeters. As you might expect from that lot, bloggers can be ruthless. A summer intern recently posted this question:

"Summering at a bb [bulge bracket, or top, investment bank], got informal feedback today from our analysts [full-time recent grads] to get some insight before official mid-summer reviews in a week. I was told I make it obvious when I'm frustrated and that I don't have a great attitude. I've never verbalized annoyance, but I suppose I don't hide it either. Don't want senior people to pick up on this. Anyone have advice as to how to appear more pleasant when you want to punch [your] associate in [the] face? I actually do like my internship, but apparently I act like I despise life or something while at work."

There were several responses, but apparently this young analyst's question hit a chord with one banker:

"That's your issue. You don't even respect authority despite the fact that you're the lowest of the low. Do whatever anyone tells you to do with a f***ing smile on your face as if you're ready to eat s***. It's a vicious circle. The more you bitch, the s***ier work you get."

Hmm . . . perhaps that was the associate who was dumping the work on that intern. His response may be strong, but it does give you an idea of how more senior colleagues might feel about the intern's attitude problem. The following is a more reflective response that fully indicates the downside of the summer analyst's behavior:

"Not sure what magical answer you're looking for—seems obvious. Just know that this is absolutely not a small thing—attitude is extremely important. When you come in FT [full time], people's technical skills (after training) will be solid and eventually everyone will be up to speed with formatting, speed, modeling, etc. such that ultimately attitude will be one of the key differentiators between analysts."

Attitude is one of those things that can hurt you if it's anything but positive. That makes sense; people know you're more productive when you're happy. They also don't like working with people who don't appear to want to be there.

Along with attitude, aptitude plays a big role in being promotable. By aptitude, I mean your capability to get the job done without appearing to self-destruct. There will be times when an incredible amount of stuff will be thrown at you. You may be working for project leaders who don't appreciate your workload from other sources, or you might have several pending deadlines in rapid succession. Sometimes you need to prioritize and even forgo an approach you might otherwise take if you had all the time in the world. These decisions will all be important factors in how you are perceived. How gracefully you get the job done will reflect on your capacity to operate under the type of stressful conditions that will multiply as you rise in your organization.

NOTE TO FILE: 

- Help stressed colleagues when you can; you both will benefit in the long run.

Chapter 2: How Others See You

Are you the Good Witch or the Bad Witch?

—Dorothy, *The Wizard of Oz*

Like any environment, the office has certain unspoken rules about the right way to communicate, dress, and act. The complicating part of the traditional office rules is that they were originated by those prehistoric professionals, the men. Way back in the day, the men just adopted the same style in the office that they followed out of the office. When professional women entered the scene in the 1970s for the first time in any kind of numbers, they didn't know if they should act like themselves or act like the men—or maybe somewhere in between. Dress was a particular problem for them as they found themselves looking like skirted mini-men in blue and gray suits. They even adopted silk bowties in the early 1980s to more exactly mimic the only role models available. Then a backlash erupted; the men didn't like women acting like men and preferred that they act like women instead. But what did that really mean? Women couldn't even think about wearing pastel sweaters in the office because they might look too feminine, or God forbid, alluring, and make the men feel uncomfortable. So the message was don't dress too masculine but don't dress too feminine either. And, by the way, the men told the women, don't try to act like us, because we're men and it's OK if we sound aggressive and commanding, because, as we said, we're men. But you can't pull that off—so you should act . . . well, we don't know how you should act. We just know how you shouldn't act.

Fortunately, the office has evolved somewhat from the 1970s and 1980s. But despite the advancement of women, there are still a significant percentage of men at the top of most organizations. So women today still have to strive to make their colleagues and clients, often mostly men, feel comfortable. For instance, can you imagine standing around with a group of men and women at your office describing the excruciating pain you felt during your recent bikini waxing? Probably not. On the other hand, you will most likely run into men at work who tell crude stories as if they were standing next to a male colleague at a urinal. Unfortunately, some things are slow to change and women still need to learn how to play the game.

Your Critical Image

For men or women, your image and conduct in the office will define you as a professional and will probably be the most important factor in your career progression. As you rise in your organization, success will begin to depend more on soft skills such as the ability to communicate effectively, create coalitions backing your ideas, and develop relationships with colleagues and clients. These are style points that you can develop during your career that all contribute to how your organization views you as a contributor. So it's important to begin to build the correct image from the moment you begin your career.

For some, developing the right professional image requires a little work. One of my former colleagues was a relaxed, imperturbable, serene type. He always got his work done without looking flustered or stressed. But as time progressed, his managers weren't sure if he would be promotable because he came off as a little too chill.

> *"He does a great job but doesn't seem to have much enthusiasm for the work."*
>
> *"Maybe he's a little lazy, just getting done what's given him."*
>
> *"He's doing a great job now, but I'm not sure he will transition well to the next step."*

The example above describes a case where my colleague's work was excellent but his image needed some polish. His lack of enthusiasm made him look like a follower, not a leader, and although he was creative, he didn't promote that ability. He needed to offer up solutions and engage more with his superiors in order to change their impressions of him.

A friend of mine in the cosmetics industry told me about a young colleague of hers who created an image problem for herself at the end of every month. Like clockwork the woman would slump down in her desk chair, moaning as she lunged for the extra-large bottle of ibuprofen at the end of her desk. Her boss began to notice and stopped grabbing her for impromptu client meetings during those periods. I wouldn't have been surprised if the manager also started forecasting her employee's menstrual cycles to avoid inviting her to meetings on certain days of the month. The woman's actions may seem insignificant but they had an impact on those around her. In the office, there's really nowhere to hide so you might as well assume your cubical walls don't exist.

During the early years of my career I had a meeting with Susan, one of my best friends from outside of work. I had gone to college with her but had never crossed paths professionally. As I watched Susan at the meeting I thought someone had invaded the body of my friend. It wasn't that I expected her to dance on the conference room table (although I had witnessed her in similar behavior outside of work). But I saw a side of Susan I hadn't seen before. It was obvious she wanted others to perceive her as a complete professional at the office. I'd say she nailed it.

Control Your Clothes

When I started my post-college job, I noticed that Hannah, one of the professional women in my office, always shimmered. Even though I was fresh out of school, I was pretty sure women didn't normally wear sequins in our line of work. Hannah was a bit clueless, but she was also probably having a tough time interpreting the rules. Don't be too masculine. Don't be too feminine. Don't make anyone feel uncomfortable. Don't make men feel too comfortable. Maybe she was trying to get noticed, knowing that shrinking into the background is a problem some women professionals have. While getting noticed is a valuable goal, in most industries you don't want to achieve it by drawing attention to your clothes.

Even if you think you know how to dress, it's a good idea to ask the Human Resources department at your company for the dress policy. They will have defined the organization's conventional business attire as well as its business casual attire. You may learn that something that looks perfectly acceptable to you and you've seen others wear (e.g., sandals in some organizations) is not permitted according to the company code. Even if you disagree, the first stage of your career is not a good time to buck the convention.

Some types of clothing choices aren't specifically spelled out in company policy. For instance, although sleeveless shirts are worn by women in most offices, they aren't the norm at higher level positions in more conservative workplaces. Subtle fashion dilemmas like those, where you don't know if you should try a burgeoning trend, are more realistically the type of questions you will have. In those situations, wait until a few other women at your level or above wear that type of clothing. That approach is not adventurous, but it's safe. And since you're in the office, not on a catwalk, it's the right decision.

If you still have questions, pick a senior woman whose style you like and don't wear anything she wouldn't wear. Maybe you can't afford a similar wardrobe, but you can replicate some knock-off pieces by shopping smartly. Of course you don't want to have to succumb to others' interpretation of style your whole career, but don't worry, as you gain in seniority you can start to impose more of your own style. I can't remember who said it, but I read a quote by a fashion icon once who reflected: *The most striking women are those who dress so well, they attract the attention, not their clothes.* That's especially great advice for the office.

There are some pieces that should be a staple in most any professional woman's wardrobe. Even if your office is casual 24/7, there will be some occasions where you'll need to attend a more formal meeting or event. Dark suits or pant and jacket separates are timeless and are easy basics to expand your wardrobe. Other essential items are a black pencil or straight skirt, office heels that you actually can walk in, and a variety of shirts to go under your jacket or blazer. To not look burdened down when your team travels from meeting to meeting, use either a small purse or a briefcase/tote bag but not both. I put a large wallet and small cosmetic-like black pouch (with keys, tissues, etc.) in my briefcase so I didn't look like I was packing to travel abroad every time I left the office. If you join a company that's office casual, select clothing pieces that not only fit in with the code but are good examples of it. For instance, if you're allowed to wear jeans, wear the smart, new-looking jeans instead of the faded, thinned-out pair hanging in your closet. Even in a casual office, it's a good idea to dress for the job you want, not the job you have.

If you are dressing for an interview, find out the company's dress code if you can. If it's business formal, then stick to a suit. If the company wears business casual then you have a little more leeway, but you should dress more formally than traditional business casual would suggest. Women are lucky because it's not an all-or-nothing situation since you don't have to make the tie/no-tie decision. You can wear dark pants or a skirt, ballet flats, a blouse or non-bulky sweater that fits under a suit jacket, and a blazer. That look will be formal enough for an interview but also fit into a more casual culture. You can always feel comfortable over-dressing in an interview (hey, they know you're dressing to impress), but never under-dress.

As you create your own style, stay away from any clothes that could be interpreted as sexy or suggestive, unless, of course, you are a professional in a type of business that's not specifically addressed in this book. Barbara Pachter, one of the leading business etiquette experts in the field, advises in her blog, *Pachter's Pointers,*[1] that among the most critical mistakes women can make in a business setting are wearing clothes that are too loose (making you look like a little girl in dress-up mode) or too tight (accenting body parts that shouldn't be highlighted), skirts that are too short and clothes that show cleavage. Also taboo is wearing a bikini when at a pool with business associates. It's sometimes hard for women professionals to understand that excessive familiarity, casualness, or exposure will change the way colleagues view them professionally. Even if you look fantastic in a bikini, that's not a judgment you want a colleague to consider if you can avoid it.

There is great up-to-date advice on the web on corporate attire for women; the following are two of my favorites. *Corporette,*[2] created by a young lawyer, offers photos of current styles and gives guidelines on everything from **whether you should wear ponytails** in the office to **how frequently you can repeat your outfits at work.** The editor at *Corporate Fashionista*[3] was exposed to many industries' styles in her job in corporate finance and gives great advice to empower the woman professional through her fashion choices.

Make-up, like the right clothes, will add to your professional image. And according to a study[4] by researchers at Harvard Medical School, Massachusetts General Hospital, Dana-Farber Cancer Institute, Procter & Gamble, and Boston University, it will make others view you as more competent and attractive than they would if you had gone without. The study also provides evidence that if you use cosmetics, you will be more likeable and considered more trustworthy.

You may have not formerly been the make-up type, but a little bit of whatever you choose—lipstick, mascara, or eye liner—will polish your professional appearance. For some women, make-up acts like a confidence boost and that's all good in the office too. Your routine shouldn't take long in the morning. It doesn't have to be a replica of the process you go through on a Saturday night, and probably shouldn't be if you tend toward more of a glamour look on weekends. Five minutes each morning ought to be enough time to tip you over into the "competent" look you're trying to achieve.

Office make-up is best if it's minimal and non-distracting. Colors should be soft and include pinks and corals for lips and browns and taupes for eyelids. You can venture away from those softer palettes as long as you pick colors that are muted and not sparkly. Red lipstick would be venturing a bit too far in most industries. Eyeliner should also be subtle and not reminiscent of Captain Jack Sparrow, no matter how confident the smoky eye look makes you feel.

NOTE TO FILE: 

- Overly feminine clothes may make you look like a baby doll, not an executive.
- If the men in your office don't look at your face when you talk, it's safe to assume you made an incorrect wardrobe choice.
- If you want to catch someone's attention, be smart, not sexy.

Once Again, in English Please

Your speech is one of the first impressions you will convey in professional situations. When you talk in the office, you should try hard not to sound like your boss's 13-year-old daughter on a trip to the mall. Skillful teenagers can replace any word that vaguely has the same meaning as "said" with "like." Really impressive ones can randomly insert "like" just about anywhere in a sentence. They make up words that never show up in the dictionary and add trendy adjectives in front of otherwise perfectly normal nouns. And, btw, acronyms are better for texting your buddies than speaking to your superiors. In other words, "OMG dude, we like, hit our numbers." should not be the way you tell your boss it was a good month.

Profanity is an interesting topic. In some offices there's a lot of it. In others, there's not. On a bond trading floor, it's a job requirement. The fact is, there's a double standard; there are men and women who are offended when women curse and not when men do. Or they believe that women can curse, but not as much as men. I think it's way too complicated to figure out. So unless you can read minds, you'll be safest to clean up your act.

Women are also accused of speaking too softly at times. If you, like me, have one of those voices that don't carry, you have to shout in loud gatherings just to be heard. But even if you're not in a noisy setting, a soft voice can come off sounding unconfident. So go big or go home; if it's worth saying, say it loudly, with confidence.

In addition to speech and word choice, improper body language can also leave the wrong impression. Social scientists have observed that women tend to touch their hair and faces frequently in the office. It's understandable. For some of us it's the first time we've been away from a mirror for more than two hours at a time. We need to make sure our faces are still there and our hair has not disappeared. But try to hold off or you won't convey the professional image that you would like.

It's useful here to point out that none of your body parts are likely to fly away and that, absent a sudden need to remove food from your chin or blow your nose, **you shouldn't touch your face.** And definitely don't twirl your hair. Don't even touch your hair. Trust me, your hair looks fabulous.

NOTE TO FILE: 

- Speak like an adult. That's about the only correct use of the word "like."
- You should generally avoid profanity unless you inadvertently drive a staple through your finger.
- Think of your hair as an erogenous zone. Don't touch it in public.

Big Girls Don't Cry

When women get upset, they sometimes become emotional and might even cry. It happens to men as well, but often they're able to channel their emotions into anger, which is more politically correct in the office. The problem is that crying makes other people feel uncomfortable, especially men, who are even uncomfortable when they are in the same room as women who are discussing heel heights. Since our professional goal is to not make anyone uncomfortable, women should not cry.

But as we know, we don't try to cry. It just happens. It doesn't happen to everyone but some just can't avoid it. If it happens to you, try to hang on to your composure as long as you can. Breathing deeply sometimes helps. I think that's why the Lamaze method was created for childbirth. With Lamaze, women can handle the pain. Therefore, they can avoid crying and making their husbands feel uncomfortable and useless.

If deep breathing doesn't work, try to remove yourself from all mankind before the dam breaks. Then you can bawl outside while walking around the office building. Lastly, if all else fails and the torrent starts, tell your superior, client, or colleague that you need a moment. If you can, try to recover quickly and return. That would be less awkward than hiding out for a few hours and then reappearing. There isn't really a perfect solution but that's as good as you can hope for under the circumstances.

NOTE TO FILE: 

- Brief hiding is OK; just don't require your company to file a Missing Persons Report.

Tame Your Inner Shrew

We should also try to avoid the stereotype of the professional female shrew. It doesn't really matter whether more angry men or women exist in the office; we have to battle against the image. So appearing calm in tense situations is especially important. It can also be disarming in an otherwise heated discussion. Luckily, women tend to be very good at it.

Joanne Conroy, CEO, Lahey Hospital and Medical Center, used her soft voice and even temper to win a battle against a raving doctor who stormed into her office at a previous job. She watched the physician's blood pressure skyrocket while she talked to him. But she knew the argument was over when he stopped pressing her on her business plan and started yelling at her for "being so damn calm."

Crisp, Clear, Concise

Another stereotype we have to overcome is that, as a gender, we talk too much. Perhaps it's true. Maybe past experience has told us that men are a little slow, so we have to repeat things. Or perhaps we have found that they tend not to listen the first time so we have to say things again. In the office though, we have to assume that our colleagues are listening. It's kind of refreshing, really.

The ability to communicate effectively through business correspondence is one of the most critical skills that a professional can possess. And internal e-mails will be a primary test of those skills. The internal e-mail explains business situations or proposals and informs, persuades, and elicits idea exchange. You should focus on writing crisp and clear e-mails without unnecessary words. Similarly, write your external letters so they are clear and on point. Review the correspondence six times, if necessary, taking out extraneous words and sharpening the text.

Your business discussions should be similar. Before you discuss even the simplest idea or proposal with senior executives, focus on what you plan to say. Write a few notes down if you need to and rehearse your dialogue in your head. Most professionals don't have excess time, and they appreciate succinct discussions that they can easily understand.

NOTE TO FILE: 

- If someone is checking their cell phone, they may no longer be listening.
- If you're afraid you can't *say* it concisely, *write* it concisely in an e-mail.
- Writing needs to be poignant and as brief as possible.
- Keep negative emotion out of all correspondence.

Kathryn Streator, co-founder of Noosphere Marketing, a digital solutions firm, told me a story about one of her first jobs at the Danbury Mint, a marketer of collectible items ranging from figurines and dolls to model cars. Kathryn typically finished her assignments quickly and was glad to be one of the first out the door. Unlike most of her co-workers, she had to reverse commute from Connecticut to Manhattan every night.

*At her first review she learned the value of **face time,** or spending time at the office, even if there's no assignment-related need to be there. In Kathryn's performance review, she was told that there was a general impression that she was always "running out early."*

"Look," her boss told her, "I know you get your work done, and you do an excellent job, but you need to realize you're creating a management dilemma for me. If you leave early, it makes it look like I'm not giving you enough work. Your peers may not catch on as quickly, but they are trying. I need to keep morale up and avoid the appearance of playing favorites. You either need to ask me for more work or ask your peers if you can help them. Kathryn, I need you to help me develop our team."

Kathryn had never considered that doing a good job might include more than simply producing quality product. That first review helped her to understand that part of performing well also meant helping her boss to be a better manager. She told me she realized after that discussion that you have to play the game and abide by unspoken office rules and culture.

If you're in one of those demanding industries where new professionals can work 80+ hour weeks, senior colleagues might encourage you to leave early (and early might mean 7 p.m.) when you get the chance. It's usually a good idea to take advantage of down time when you normally have a crazy schedule. But if it's been calm for you recently, realize that staying late may give you an opportunity to help some senior officers if unscheduled work pops up. Or you might have an opportunity to interact with associates who are normally too busy during the day to connect. You can probably check over your own work again anyway so sticking around won't be a waste of your time.

Act the Expert

As your career develops, colleagues, clients, and superiors will assume you know more than you do. Now, to continue fooling them, it's important to learn how to reply to questions when you have no idea how to answer. I listened to an exchange once between two naval officers giving a tour of a U.S. destroyer. When someone asked a question about the navigation system, one of the officers replied that he didn't know the answer. I heard the second officer take him aside and say, "Dude, if you don't know the answer, just tell them it's classified information."

I'm not suggesting you bluff your way through your career but you don't have to look like a deer in headlights every time you don't know an answer. Much of the time, your colleagues don't know answers either. Often your superiors or their clients will be satisfied if you tell them how you will find the answer, such as "That depends on sales growth in blah blah blah, which I can find out from my colleagues in the blah blah blah department. I'll investigate it and get back to you." That response makes you sound thoughtful, not ignorant. You can also answer a slightly different question from the one posed. You probably perfected that technique back in high school after coming home late from parties.

We're All Adults Here

One time I tried calling my naval officer father by his first name, and he quickly warned me that I was "bordering on insubordination." No joke. I wanted to laugh, but even at age 13, I wasn't that stupid. With my upbringing as a Navy brat, I entered the workforce with as much fear of corporate brass as anyone else.

At my first job, my cubicle was next to a veteran of two years named Garrett. I figured he already knew the lay of the land so I asked him a burning question: What should I call senior officers, in particular the one I am supposed to meet with in an hour?

"What do I call him? Mr. Evans? Sir?"

"No," Garrett responded. "You call all 3,000 people at this firm by their first name, including the CEO."

"No way. I can't"

"What do you mean, you can't?"

"It's disrespectful."

"What? You're crazy. If you call him 'Mr. Evans,' he won't take you seriously. You need to make him realize you are a professional, a colleague, an equal...well, sort of. And for God's sake, don't call him 'Sir.' You'll make him feel old as crap and then he definitely won't want to work with you."

I didn't believe him. This had to be a trick to make the new trainee look stupid. I still sat at the kids table at Thanksgiving; how could I call a man my father's age by his first name? But eventually, I realized that, in the office, I was one of the adults and that showing too much respect for senior officers would emphasize the gap between their seniority and my lowliness. That gap was way too obvious to me already; I didn't need to highlight it.

Most U.S. companies have the same standard but it would be worthwhile to check with a veteran about your company's customs. Internationally, the workforce tends to be more formal. As a junior officer, I became the primary interface for a British CEO, called Mr. Maxwell by all of his employees, no matter how senior they were. I felt like I had been liberated by my earlier advice to call everyone in my company by their first name, so I was confused as to how I should address him. At one point, after several meetings together, I just asked him. "You can call me Bob," he said. Phew, I thought, he gets it. He understands how my company operates and is allowing me to follow the American convention.

The title question comes into play in correspondence as well. During the job application phase of your career you'll likely write to a number of people whom you've never met. It's appropriate to address the correspondence with the recipient's title: Mr., Ms., Dr., etc. If you receive correspondence back from someone who signs only their first name, with their address block below, you can henceforth and evermore address them by their first name in person and in correspondence. And make sure you do. The respondent is telling you that "we're both professionals, let's get on with it." You might even make him feel uncomfortable if you continue to address him by his surname.

The Corner on Guilt

Have you noticed when men drive and they make a mistake, it's always someone else's fault? "Damn car! He got right in my blind spot!" Of course he did. No operator error there. Men have built-in ego-preservation mechanisms that allow them to function well on the roadway and in the office. They make a mistake, they move on. When women make a mistake, however, they beat themselves up. In an office environment, women need to let go. Everyone messes up. Now get over it!

If you have discovered a mistake you made that will change an outcome or a presentation, tell your colleagues who are affected by the error and offer a plan to correct it. You don't need to be overly apologetic or remorseful, and certainly don't get emotional or your associates may become embarrassed. Depending on the size of the error, you might want to indicate that you will take steps to avoid making a similar mistake again.

But don't assume you've made a mistake if you haven't. If you're not completely happy with the analysis you wrote, there is no need to apologize to your manager before he reads it. He may love it. And if he tells you he does, don't tell him you weren't sure if the section on blah blah blah was any good. It was good. He just told you.

Chivalry or Chauvinism?

Are you appreciative when a man holds out his hand as you exit from a cab? Or do you wonder if the guy thinks you're going to fall smack down on your butt without his help? Who does he think you are, some prissy little debutante? My suggestion is to take his hand, say thank you, and move on. I guarantee, whoever it is—client, boss, subordinate, or mail room boy—you will make him feel like a gentleman. And frankly, we could use a few more of those in this world. Whenever a man makes a gesture that you believe is archaic and demeaning, he's most likely attempting to be helpful and may be embarrassed if you don't accept his assistance. There is no point in chastising the man when he's just doing what his mother taught him to do.

Similarly, be polite when a man or woman compliments you. I've heard men say that women don't know how to accept compliments at the workplace and are sometimes rude in response. The women don't mean to be discourteous; they just don't know how they should respond. The rules in this case are the same as outside work; if someone compliments you, don't disagree. When you graciously accept the compliment, whether it's about your work, your look, or anything else about you, three things happen:

1. You confirm your complimenter's perception.
2. You leave your complimenter thinking you are confident and secure.
3. You make your complimenter feel good.

NOTE TO FILE: 

- You can compliment, too. Whether they're senior or junior executives, everyone likes to hear confirmation that their presentation went well.

Push for the Podium

A national television reporter initially had a tough time getting traction in a particularly cut-throat industry. "I took stand-up comedy lessons," she told me. "That way, a bad hair day just became material." Thankfully, we're not all in the spotlight around the clock but most of us could benefit from gaining experience in public speaking. Even at a junior level, you might have opportunities to give industry presentations. Your boss may be looking to offload some of his own trade show or industry panel responsibilities. Tell him you're interested in presenting and ask if there are any opportunities. With increased presentation experience, you'll gain exposure within your industry and develop poise and confidence addressing public forums. As a result, your boss will likely begin to rely on you more for independent assignments.

Image Brush-Up

If the thought of public speaking is terrifying to you, then you might need help. Many companies offer training for employees seeking to develop themselves professionally. If your manager has identified an issue or you believe you have an area that needs developing, be proactive about your improvement before the problem begins to impede your advancement. Ask your manager how you would go about getting the training. And if she can't provide you with any information, contact your Human Resources department. Representatives from HR should be able to help you with internal training programs or refer you to outside public speaking, career, and leadership coaches. Even if you have to pay out of pocket, investing in professional coaching could have a big impact on your career by helping you in areas that may be hampering your advancement.

Notable businessman and philanthropist Warren Buffett has spoken about his efforts to polish his image. He was terrified of public speaking all throughout college and into the early years of his career. Even though he enrolled in a Dale Carnegie course, the gold standard for teaching effective communication and relationship skills for business, Buffett couldn't even bear attending the class. He didn't show up and cancelled payment on his check. Buffett later explained in an interview[5] on Levo League's Levo.com that he had come to the realization that he just couldn't go through life that way. So he decided to enroll again in the course, this time paying in cash. "The class changed my life in a big way," Buffett reflected; it helped him gain the confidence to speak to groups. And to make sure that the progress he had made didn't start to recede after finishing the Carnegie course, Buffett immediately applied to teach a night course at the University of Omaha.

Calculated Conduct

Is it appropriate to drink at lunch? Who eats first at a business dinner? When I'm in a taxi with an associate, who pays? How do I interpret a married male colleague asking me for a lunch? What do I say if my manager always asks me to get him coffee? How do you figure this stuff out? Unfortunately, you just can't ask Siri.

It's important to get a handle on office decorum when you first begin working. Many times, simply observing executives' behavior will educate you about acceptable office practices; sometimes you need to ask an office veteran.

Office Charm School

Although some situations arise in the office that don't occur in the outside world, you should generally follow the same etiquette in your workplace as you do out of it. So make sure you know the rules of common etiquette, and you'll succeed in both environments.

My friend Kate thought she had the rules under control until she interviewed for a job in New York City. The French-American businessman she was to meet invited her to lunch at a restaurant near his office. Kate met her interviewer and chatted with him easily as they looked over the menu. Her eyes darted from dish to dish trying to find the easiest one to eat while answering questions. She settled on some sort of white fish. When it arrived, she sprinkled a little salt on it and took her first bite. As expected, she didn't really like it, but it allowed her to swallow quickly and talk more freely. The lunch went well and Kate was sold on the company by the time she shook hands to say goodbye. She was hoping for an offer within a few days but instead she received a ding letter. The rejection was not what she was expecting; she thought she had aced the interview. Kate then uncovered more details from a friend of hers at the company. Apparently, the French businessman took his etiquette seriously. She fell out of the competition for the job when she salted her food before she tasted it.

Not all executives will reject you for premature salt application. The safest strategy, however, is to know the basic standards of etiquette to avoid being mistaken for a hillbilly by anyone. Ask your mother, ask your roommate, read up on etiquette, but make sure you know the rules.

Two websites I like for quick access to etiquette tips are *Pachter's Pointers,*[6] mentioned earlier, by Barbara Pachter, a business etiquette expert, and *Emily Post,*[7] a site carrying on the work of the pioneer in chronicling American manners. Ms. Post's heirs, who now manage the Emily Post Institute, cover all aspects of etiquette, including appropriate behaviors ranging from businesses to weddings.

There's also commonsense protocol that may not expressly be stated in an etiquette manual but which you can pick up by keeping your eyes open. No matter how casual your office environment, you'll notice there will be some hierarchical differences in the protocol for junior and senior employees. In a customer meeting, let your boss sit next to, or across from, the client. If you are the junior employee, jump into the uncomfortable middle seat in the car ride, even if you're five inches taller than your colleague.

NOTE TO FILE: 

- Use your outside utensil first; bread and salad are to the left, water and wine to the right.
- The most senior host of the meal, or the client, takes the first bite.

- Stand up, make eye contact, and shake hands when you meet someone.
- Shake it, girl; give strong handshakes and stand tall.
- You never have to drink alcohol at lunch. Avoid it completely if a drink affects you. In any case, one is enough.
- Don't chew gum in a meeting or while walking around the office. If you're hunkered down at your computer, it's OK.

Know Thy Company

Before I understood that my work environment might have different rules from those I grew up with, I made a mistake that a senior officer pointed out to me. She saw me exiting a taxi as my client had just finished paying the driver and whispered, "Why didn't you pay?"

I don't know why I didn't pay. I guess the guy reminded me of my father; he talked like my father; he even looked like my father. I'm thankful I didn't ask him for my weekly allowance. It certainly didn't occur to me to pay for the taxi; my father always did that.

When you begin work at a new organization, you need to observe and to ask questions. Ask a peer who has been at the company a while or a more senior employee to explain the company protocol. Should you give a gift to your assistant or a client during the holidays? What type of gift is appropriate? How much should you spend? Can you accept a gift from a client? Will you be reimbursed if you take your junior colleague out to lunch to celebrate the completion of a project? Can you ask your assistant to make personal reservations for you? You'll find Human Resources will supply some of the answers, but for others you'll just have to ask around. In any case, don't underestimate your woman's intuition. If doing something doesn't feel right, it probably isn't.

It's also important to understand the practices and customs of your clients and customers. Sometimes, learning the hard way is the only option, or at least that's what a business school graduate named Annie discovered.

Annie graduated in a tough job market and rather reluctantly joined an East Coast supplier of factory systems to the dairy industry. Annie's job was to sell machines that milked cows, processed the milk, and then inserted the milk into vacuum-packed aseptic containers. Her client base was Midwest dairy farmers.

Annie had never actually aspired to sell factory equipment that required knowledge of cow udder tolerances. She was also pretty sure that she was the only member of her graduating business school class who had to wear a hair net during product demonstrations. But the most dreaded aspect of her new job was the requirement of socializing with good-old-boy dairy farmers in Kansas.

On Annie's first sales call, she pretended to enjoy her tour of the customer's dairy plant despite her fear that she would spike a cow paddy with one of her heels and carry it with her for the rest of the afternoon. When noon approached, Annie was grateful she could get off the farm. She just needed to take the two dairy men to lunch and she could head for the airport. As she sat down on that brutally hot day and ordered lemonade, she wondered how quickly she could be on her way without appearing rude.

But to her shock, time seemed to fly by. She even started to have fun.

"Unbelievable!" Annie thought. "These farm boys aren't so bad after all! In fact, I'm actually enjoying myself!"

"I bet my sissy-assed city friends aren't having as much fun as I am!" Annie said a little too loudly to her new customers.

Annie decided, after two tall lemonades, that she needed to visit the restroom. But as she stood up, she became aware that somehow she had become totally wasted. Just when she was trying to figure out who put vodka in her lemonade she took an unsuccessful step and, in a panic, realized that she was falling to the ground. Annie lunged for a wall sconce, missed it, and tried to grasp the table edge but grabbed her customer's knee instead. She continued to fly sideways, bottoms up, across his lap.

Annie's clients were gracious and only brought up her lap dive five times during her subsequent visit. She learned from the experience that when you take Midwest dairy farmers to lunch, unless you specify, lemonade is made with Absolut Citron.

The Girl Duties

Women are particularly talented in several areas: serving coffee, planning office parties, nurturing young trainees, resolving administrative assistant squabbles, and organizing junior work assignments. It's so fabulous that we possess these unique talents. If they just didn't hinder all the other work we have to get done.

Let's start first with serving coffee. Believe it or not, there are some old-school bosses who still ask the female trainee to serve coffee at a meeting. Let's assume for the moment that your boss is savvy enough not to saddle you with such a cliché task. Instead he asks you to perform another, not so obviously sexist one: to clean up the conference room between meetings. If you're the only junior employee involved, it's not an outrageous request. However, if you're standing next to an able-bodied male peer at the time, you would be right to suspect chauvinism. In that case, it's legitimate for you to say, "Hey Liam, want to give me a hand?"

Hopefully you successfully sent a discreet message to your boss that cleaning up is really not a female-specific duty. If, alternatively, you aren't able to subtly convey to your boss that his suggestion reeks of blatant sexism, go ahead and clean up the conference room. Making a scene would not win you any fans. Who knows, maybe he made a single senseless mistake that he will never repeat. If that's not the case and your boss continues to ask you to do all of the clean-up, talk to him alone. Explain that, though you are happy to help out, you believe that fulfilling the stereotypical girl duties may damage your professional reputation. There's a good chance your boss didn't realize the mistake he was making and will understand your concern.

Being asked to do the girl duties is clearly infuriating and humiliating. What's even worse though is that your colleagues are also forming an image of you as the trainee who pours the coffee, cleans up the conference room, or takes the lunch order. Historically, these tasks were filled by non-executive-track employees. You don't want your colleagues to make that association with you, no matter how subliminal.

When I was a summer intern I didn't need my boss to subordinate my image at the company. I managed to handle that job all by myself. I was in his office once when a distress call came in from his wife. Her babysitter had canceled, and she didn't know how she was going to find coverage before she had to meet him. Before I knew it, I had volunteered to watch my boss's kids. That's me, always trying to be helpful. And I was. But for the rest of the summer my boss never looked at me the same way. I think he was trying to figure out whether I'd be more valuable as a babysitter or an employee.

Even if you don't compromise your own image like I did, it's important to realize that seemingly beneficial projects at work can negatively impact your career. Every non-core business activity you perform means you have less time available for your primary work.

I worked in an industry where there were plenty of opportunities for women to take on work that wouldn't necessarily enhance their careers. In investment banking, financial analysts, directly out of college, are divided into specialty groups headed by senior bankers. Analysts are assigned deals within each group by the *assignments associate,* generally an MBA who has gained enough experience to be able to determine how much work each analyst can take on. It's quite an honor to be appointed assignments associate within your group. It means that senior bankers believe you can handle your own workload as well as manage the analyst pool.

At my bank, I noticed there were more women assignments associates than men. The senior execs must have realized that the young women bankers were better multi-taskers and better managers of the analysts, often just two years their junior, than the men.

It wasn't until I was a senior investment banker that a female peer, formerly an assignments associate, explained that despite the honor of being asked to take on the management role, the job itself really compromised her career. She explained that she worked non-stop trying to keep up with the demands of managing the analysts and completing her own work. But when a premier deal came in the door, the head of her group would award it to another associate who he knew had the time to devote to it. As a result, after a one-year stint as assignments associate, my colleague's deals generated fewer revenues than did her peers' deals.

"At the end of the day," she stated, "I was considered a great manager who produced good revenues. Many of my peers were considered good managers who produced great revenues. Guess which of us were considered more valuable?"

Leadership and teamwork may be highly valued in your organization, enough so that extra duties are net benefits to your record. But to determine the right mix, you need to be constantly aware of how non-core functions can influence your work product or the perception of your value at your company. Not all companies have the same criteria for success. What are the criteria at your company? Revenues? Market share? Product innovation? Leadership initiatives? Client quality? Is the added task high profile within the firm? Will it diminish your ability to perform your core job? Will you receive a different quality of core assignments? Will the new function change your interaction with key executives? Will the additional responsibility affect your compensation or standing at the company? A new responsibility could be the best thing for your career, just make sure you consider all aspects before you undertake it.

NOTE TO FILE: 

- Are there more women than men assigned to certain types of jobs? Is there a reason that you can identify?
- If you think someone is repeatedly treating you in a sexist manner, and your efforts haven't produced any changes, ask a senior female professional who you trust how to deal with it. If it crosses the boundaries of minor infractions, discuss it with Human Resources.

Sexual Politics

It can be uncomfortable for women in offices who feel that they can't be themselves and joke with their colleagues the way they would with a friend. These women crank back their personalities for fear they might be perceived as coming on to someone. Being cautious in the beginning is the best way to get to know your colleagues and to make sure you aren't misinterpreted. What may seem neighborly behavior to one guy might seem flirtatious behavior to another. So office conduct will be one of those feel-your-way-through situations (not literally, please!). Eventually, as you begin to get to know the cast of characters in your office, you'll figure out how to safely interact with each of them, without sending the wrong messages.

When I had been at my first job about six months, Peter, an associate in Mergers and Acquisitions, told me he would like to talk to me about working on a transaction. I was a generalist in investment banking, had never had an opportunity to work on an M&A deal, and was excited about the prospect. Those projects were known to be secretive, fast-paced, and highly dramatic when bids for companies were negotiated or rejected.

When I met Peter, he began to talk to me about my role. I knew M&A was the closest I was going to get to feeling like a character in a television suspense drama, but I thought Peter's emphasis on secrecy was a little excessive. He repeatedly told me during the conversation that I could talk to no one about this transaction, especially any other banker in M&A because they might be working on a deal with an industry competitor. Peter added that it would be dangerous to even say I'm working on an M&A transaction because I might inadvertently slip up. The more I heard Peter's warnings, the more I began to worry. I was secretly dating an M&A banker. We knew inter-office relationships weren't the best idea, so we kept ours hidden. I feared Peter would find out about the relationship, be furious, and kick me off the deal. If that happened, I was sure my reputation would suffer. As I listened I decided I had to come clean. "Peter, I have to tell you something," I said. "I'm dating Chris."

"Are you kidding me?" Peter responded. "You think I don't know that? That's why I'm stressing secrecy so much."

My relationship at that point was a secret to probably no one. Office dating is a practice everyone knows they should avoid. Yet, according to an annual Careerbuilder.com study,[8] 39% of workers have admitted to an inter-office romance at least once in their career. We just don't seem to be able to control ourselves. Of course, inter-office dating would be viewed completely differently if the couples never broke up. Having to work with someone who you would prefer to see die a slow death is really quite unpleasant. Even if you're the breaker, not the breakee, who wants to deal with a barrage of guilt, remorse, temptation, disgust, or whatever other emotions might come into play when you are constantly reminded of your ex?

The scenarios that you should try to avoid entirely are the situations where you begin dating your boss or a subordinate. Not only is there the potential for break-up trauma, but it's likely that one of you will be accused of favoritism, poor judgment, and **sleeping your way to the top.** At the very least you will become the subject of gossip that could change your relationship with your co-workers, create an unfavorable image of you, and possibly get you fired. Is anyone really worth that?

Discretion Is the Better Part of Everything

Women should be interesting enough that their colleagues would want to have a beer with them after work. Not a double martini. That's a different kind of interesting. That's not to say that you have to have a beer with any particular associate; you just want them to want to have a beer with you.

Men have much more latitude in bringing their outside, social self into the office. They can boast about their ability to slam down shots of tequila to an admiring audience of office mates. If a women makes the same claim, her colleagues immediately think that she's an alcoholic, lacks judgment, demonstrates risky behavior, or perhaps worse, is unfeminine.

And then there's the office party. The first decision you must make is what to wear. If the party is on a Saturday night, away from the office, you don't have to wear business attire but make sure whatever you pick is classy, not campy. If the party is on a weeknight and everyone is leaving from the office, don't change your clothes. Wear something to work that's a little nicer than usual, but still conservative.

One year I saw a professionally attired woman going into the ladies room and emerging in a hot little dress, six-inch heels, and make-up as thick as my keyboard. She got plenty of attention that night but in the following weeks couldn't figure out why her relationship with her co-workers had changed. Everyone saw her in a different light and had that image in their mind during the work day.

At another office event, one woman in my office drank so much that her boss and another associate had to take her home in a cab. The two men carried her up three flights of stairs in her brownstone apartment and laid her down on her bed. Before they left they propped her up on her side so she wouldn't choke if she vomited.

All the details of this adventure had spread around the office before the woman had woken up the next day. And the story followed her around for years, even after she switched companies.

Even if you're discreet about your work wardrobe and social habits, you can still get into trouble talking about those of others—or virtually anything else you say about your colleagues. Remember middle school? The office can be kind of like that, but often the consequences are much worse. If you say something negative about somebody, it has a way of taking form and traveling around the office, even if you told your office mate *in confidence*. That crap just happens. It happened when you were 13; it will happen now. That's why sisters, uncles, BFFs, and anyone else you trust outside of the office exist; so you can gripe about your colleagues and not have it damage your career.

There are lots of other taboo behaviors that are worthwhile mentioning. They include any sort of cosmetic application at your desk including nail polish, eye shadow, and especially perfume. If you're going out after work, stop in the restroom on the way out.

I had lunch once with a male colleague and a potential client. The client was in the middle of a sentence when she reached into her purse, pulled out a tube of lipstick, applied it, put it back in her purse, and kept talking. She was the hoped-for client so she could have drawn clown lips on her face and we wouldn't have flinched. She did make us both uncomfortable though. We didn't know where to look.

There are forbidden subjects as well, and subjects that the guys just don't want to hear about: weight, diets, hair treatments, visits to your analyst, fights with your partner, attempts to become pregnant. Go ahead and tell your colleagues that you started running every day. Don't tell them that your partner dumped you because you gained fifteen pounds so you need to start running.

NOTE TO FILE:

- Applying make-up at your desk is as appropriate as applying deodorant at a bus stop.
- Unless you want to hear about their E.D., don't talk about your P.M.S.

How Do You Recognize Sexual Harassment?

An ABC/Washington Post survey[9] found that one in four women polled said they had experienced sexual harassment in the workplace. With the incidence of sexual harassment significant enough that it will likely affect you or somebody you know, it's a good idea to understand what signifies harassment and what you should do about it. **Harassment occurs when behavior is sufficiently severe or pervasive to create a hostile work environment or result in a tangible change at work such as failure to promote.** Simple teasing, offhand comments, or isolated minor incidents would not qualify as harassment.

Examples of actions that may create a hostile environment are:

- Staring in a sexually suggestive manner
- Making offensive remarks about looks, clothing, or body parts
- Making repetitive unsolicited advances
- Touching in a way that may make an employee feel uncomfortable
- Telling sexual or lewd jokes, hanging sexual posters, or making sexual gestures
- Sending, forwarding, or soliciting sexually suggestive letters, notes, e-mails, or images

A potential threat can emanate from within or outside the firm. Managers, co-workers, customers, contractors, or vendors can all be responsible for sexual harassment. If behavior from one of these individuals is making you uncomfortable, your first action should be to ask him to stop. If the situation persists, the Human Resources department is your safe haven; HR professionals know how to assess the behavior and advise you on the best strategy. Unfortunately, the majority of harassed employees don't report incidents for fear of retaliation, worries their co-workers will make them feel ashamed by the experience, and other concerns. In the ABC/Washington Post poll mentioned previously, only 41% of those harassed reported the offense to their employers.

Encouragingly, that percentage is trending the right way; 34% reported incidents in a similar poll conducted seventeen years earlier. HR departments are getting better at educating their employees about behavior that is considered harassment. And companies are less tolerant than they were in years past of employees creating these hostile environments. If ever you are confused about what tact you should take in the event of potential harassment, remember: your company is legally responsible for guaranteeing you a safe work environment.

Navigating Foreign Lands

Women experience a unique set of challenges working abroad. And Americans are comparatively provincial when it comes to understanding other nations' customs. They don't have the constant exposure to a variety of cultures experienced certainly by their European and often their Latin American and Asian counterparts.

Some professionals may wonder if they should even pursue work in a field that might require knowledge of a foreign language they don't know. They should really find out what the specific requirements are before they discount their chances. I once asked the former head of Latin American Investment Banking at Merrill Lynch if he spoke Spanish or Portuguese and he told me he didn't. He explained, "If the potential clients don't speak English, their companies are probably not significant enough businesses for us to pursue." Clearly his understanding was based on his seniority and his firm's target market. He did have a large staff of Hispanic speakers who reported to him but there were also bankers with no Spanish or Portuguese training. So experience level, playing field, and internal demand have a bearing on whether you will need to learn a language. The banker told me that he was taking beginning Spanish lessons because, to him, having an understanding of the language was like playing client golf. "You may not need to play to win business, but you learn more about your client if you do."

When you're planning to work abroad, ask others about the cultural differences in the office, or if possible, get intelligence on specific team members and clients. If your foreign client or colleague has specific hot buttons, that information could be helpful to learn ahead of time. I know now that I should have dialed it back a notch when I dealt with an Argentinean private equity investor who was uncomfortable with confident women professionals. You don't have to agree with a foreigner's value system to realize you can moderate your approach to further a relationship.

There may come a time when a female ex-pat needs to decide how to react when she becomes involved in behavior that's, well, un-American. I remember scooting over to London on the last flight I could take before my daughter was born. With an obvious six-month bump, I was taken off-guard when my new British client asked whether I minded if he smoked. "What? Are you bloody kidding me?" I wanted to say, but instead told him to go ahead. In my altered state at the time, I was sure I was going to bear a child with lung cancer. That was my fault. I could have said, "No problem, I'll just move over a bit." My client wasn't being malicious, England just had different standards; a British friend of mine was pregnant at the same time and her doctor told her to cut back to one pack a day. At a different time, I was the banker for a Czech Republic client who asked me to "take a letter." I didn't get it. "Take it where?" I asked. "No, no . . . write this down" he said. Oh... he wanted to dictate to me, 1950s style. "Just a minute," I said, "I'll get my assistant."

Working abroad or even at home with colleagues and clients from elsewhere requires you to contend with issues that won't likely arise in the United States. Rules of etiquette may be similar across borders but one country may emphasize specific issues more than another country. And just as we judge foreigners for behavior we think is inappropriate, they will do the same to us. The most successful business people study the customs of the culture they'll be exposed to before they arrive. If you are about to begin working with professionals outside of the U.S., be prepared and find yourself a cultural mentor, or two or three, to guide you on your way.

Cyber Sensible

E-mail has made businesses much more efficient. But office e-mailing can drag you down when you have to wade through useless e-mails. Some executives complain that they receive 300 to 500 e-mails a day and wish their offices would cut down on unnecessary messages. It's a good personal goal to have, too, because if you e-mail excessively or are too wordy, then colleagues may tend to skim or discard an e-mail they see with your name on it. You want to be one of those professionals who add value with each e-mail. You also need to be careful about clicking the *Reply* and *Reply All* buttons. If you are adding value, it's worthwhile. If you are searching for the electronic equivalent of face time, you may just be annoying people.

E-mails are also a dangerous medium when emotions are running high. If someone really made you mad, it's better to calmly discuss the matter with her. If you choose to e-mail instead, strip any emotion out of your correspondence. Anger in an e-mail tends to be magnified by 10. Plus, your adversary now has a written record of your testy response. Before you send an e-mail you're not sure about, you may want a confidante to read it to make sure it conveys no negative emotions. In any case, avoid using all caps or exclamation points to highlight a point. That is the equivalent of electronic shouting. At the very least, wait half an hour, or better yet, 24 hours before you hit the *Send* button.

If you're on the receiving end, the same rules apply. I recently received an e-mail response which started out "*As I stated in my previous e-mail . . .*" OK, my bad for just skimming the earlier e-mail, but did she have to start out like that? I wanted to lob back my version of a passive-aggressive response because I didn't like her attitude. But I've been in enough of those situations to know that I needed to stomp down my inner 4-year-old and act pleasant in response. At least I hoped she might feel guilty after she received my mature response.

Some e-mails are unintentionally grumpy. A friend of mine calls them *man-mails* because she thinks that men often send terse, straightforward messages. They're not meant to be brusque; they probably just don't reread their e-mails and realize how curt they sound. Or, your correspondent may be busy and just attempting to quickly clear his inbox. I read an article about a woman who e-mailed her boss a six-point strategy she planned to follow on her project. He e-mailed back, "Noted." His short response made her think he was mad and she called him right away. He told her he wasn't angry, he just knew she was on top of the assignment and was trying to dispense with the e-mail quickly.

E-mail chains with two sides offering opposing views create a whole new set of issues. After about the fourth impassioned e-mail exchange on a particular topic I just start skimming the content, trying to miss all the unnecessary histrionics. So when a writer offers just the facts, as if she's trying to be impartial, I tend to pay more attention. In most of these situations, though, that unemotional e-mail often sways the reader because the writer can clearly choose which facts to present. Without all the white noise surrounding most of the other communications on the issue, the reader will tend to focus on those facts. So choose your words wisely. Sometimes the most impassioned speech will drive your potential proponents away when a short dispassionate display of the facts will win them over.

I was in an e-mail exchange recently where a writer who disagreed with me felt like she wasn't making enough headway. She added three people to the e-mail chain and restated her thoughts. Unfortunately for her, two of the newcomers didn't support her points, causing the discussion to end quickly. The woman should have made sure she knew where everyone stood on her issue before she brought it online. That rule can apply to many types of discussions and is the practice board members follow before they bring up topics at a board of directors meeting.

Other electronic-media-related discourteous behavior includes paying too much attention to your cell phone, tablet, or other electronic device while you are in a meeting or having a conversation with a colleague. Please wait until after you have finished your meeting or your conversation to text, e-mail, or otherwise ignore your colleagues. If you are expecting a critical phone call while you are in a meeting, give your mobile to your administrative assistant and ask him to interrupt you.

Similarly, speaking on a cell phone while in a taxi with colleagues has its own set of rules. If you are the senior officer, you can use your phone freely; just remember that those junior colleagues won't miss a word of your conversation. If you are a junior professional and there are senior colleagues in a taxi, keep personal calls to a minimum; they are distracting to others and occasionally inappropriate.

Electronic security is probably the most important e-related issue you need to be aware of in the office. It's very possible that your e-mails, website searches, social network posts, and shopping history are under review at your company. In some offices, even direct supervisors have access to the e-mails sent by their employees. Nor should you trust the privacy of sending an e-mail on your personal account from your office computer. If it's an office computer, techies can view everything you've written. In fact, even if your device doesn't belong to your organization, if you are tapping into your company's internet, it can tap into your every electronic movement. One technology specialist at a health-care company told me his staff intercepts all communications with certain words and strings of numbers of certain length. The organization is clamping down on profanity and security breaches. The words are triggers for non-businesslike correspondence as well as patient privacy information that shouldn't escape the system.

As far as your own privacy, just pretend the *Delete* button isn't there. Your message never really disappears. Not long ago, you could at least take a sledge hammer to your hard drive and your company's data storage equipment to eliminate all traces of internet activity. Now with companies storing on the Cloud, your past communications are saved even farther from you with no possibility of taking back what you once transmitted. E-mails and other documents are also stored on company printers. Every picture taken can be accessed for litigation or other purposes by your company. As my technology specialist friend told me, "There's no way to hide anything."

Though not connected to the internet, the office telephone may not be much more secure. Depending on the industry, some employee phone calls are recorded. In those cases, the employee is generally warned by the company that calls may be monitored or recorded. The employee is not warned, however, when a colleague or assistant decides to pick up her line outside of her office and listen in after pushing the *Mute* button.

And although you haven't asked your boss to be your *Friend* on Facebook or accepted her as a follower on Twitter, Instagram, Vine, or any other website or app, assume that she, as well as other senior officers, clients, subordinates, and the Human Resources department at your company, can view your profile, blogs, and comments. If you wouldn't want them reading something, you need to keep it off the internet. Even if your social network pages are squeaky clean, do your friends have pictures of you engaged in less-than-professional behavior on their networks? If so, you should ask them to delete them.

Diane Paddison, Chief Strategy Officer of Cassidy Turley, told me a story of blogging gone wrong. Diane is a member of a national women's real estate organization that has helped boost its participants' careers. She described Sydney, a rising star in the industry, who was chosen to be one of 10 participants in the group's mentor program. After the initial kick-off meeting, Sydney blogged about the lack of brokers involved in the organization. Sydney was trying to initiate a discussion, but the organization's board members viewed her piece as harsh criticism. Some were ready to ask her to resign from the program. Diane stepped in, talked to Sydney about the impact of the article, and asked her to pull it. "She had her facts wrong, which angered those who were supposed to be her allies. It wasn't a circumspect thing to do," Diane observed.

Lastly, you should be aware of a new trend increasingly adopted by organizations. It's the remote *wiping* of cell phones when an employee quits or is terminated. Though the phone may be owned and paid for by the employee, some companies argue that the phone contains work-related information to which they have rights. These companies' employees are given information when they join the organization, which indicates that the wiping may occur, but for many of the new hires that message does not stand out in a mass of employee material. If you're unsure whether your company will wipe your phone clear of not only work-related information but also personal contacts, photos, e-mails, and other data, it's a good idea to back it up often, just in case.

NOTE TO FILE:

- Think of every digital correspondence as your legacy. It may be around a lot longer than you are.

Chapter 3: Plotting a Course

Without leaps of imagination, or dreaming, we lose the excitement of possibilities. Dreaming, after all, is a form of planning.

—Gloria Steinem

My husband was CEO of an industrial products company when one of his junior employees asked him to help her figure out her career path. "I wish it were that simple," Jon responded. "There's no career path anymore; no definitive route to ensure you reach your career goal. Instead, focus on skill acquisition. There are certain skills that are necessary for the job you want to have in ten years. Let's talk about those."

The notion of the career path that our society developed in the '50s, '60s, and '70s, where professionals worked in few companies and progressed in predictable corporate patterns, isn't relevant for Millennial workers. Industry and organizational structures have changed and professionals' desire to become lifers at their

first companies has also changed. And perhaps most importantly, since the technology boom in 2002, the creation of jobs that didn't exist in past generations means that there may not be a good proxy for advancement in your particular field.

Instead of trying to find a path to follow, today's most successful professionals seek to acquire the right skills to set themselves up for advancement. C-suite executives, where the most senior executives of an organization reside, often have acquired a variety of skills which will be useful in their specific function as well as in their role as advisor to the board, the CEO, or other senior colleagues. These executives seek positions that will give them the varied experiences where they can gain those skills. When a professional takes on a job as CFO of an unprofitable division, she not only acquires financial and management skills to add to her arsenal but also important turnaround skills that can be applied in many situations going forward.

If you plan to eventually start your own company, you especially need to focus on skill acquisition. Defying the norm are Silicon Valley entrepreneurs like Mark Zuckerberg of Facebook and Bill Gates of Microsoft, who both began to build their companies after dropping out of Harvard University. Most mere mortals benefit from gaining exposure to different operational areas within established companies and also developing the management skills of leading employees, which can be the most challenging skills to perfect.

But whether you plan to stay in your company for the long haul or eventually leave to start your own, you have to first determine if you are in the right company and the right industry. Many new professionals aren't completely sure. I went from investment banking to consumer product marketing back to investment banking before I figured out that finance was for me. If you are launching your career or would like to shift out of one that you began, you can find out more about your options through career assessments and informational discussions. Assessments, either self-administered or conducted by a service, give you a perspective on your interests, character strengths, personality type, and goals as they relate to possible career choices. Recruitment professionals swear by these tools saying the evaluations direct users toward the types of careers where they'll perform the best and be the happiest. Many company human resource managers require applicants to take some form of these tests to determine if they will fit well within their organization.

Connecting with friends, colleagues, alumni networks, industry contacts, and business organization members will all help you vet different types of jobs and fields and direct you toward the one to pursue. If you haven't figured out what direction you need to go, you probably haven't talked to enough people. There's at least one ideal career for everyone, you just need to do the research to find out which one is right for you.

Reassessing your career periodically is helpful even when you're not switching jobs. Make sure you have been in your job long enough to understand the opportunities ahead of you and then take stock of your fit within the field. Younger employees can be influenced by the menial work they're assigned, so it's important to realize that grunt work exists in many entry-level professions. The more revealing consideration is whether you believe the job three levels ahead of you would be exciting. If so, you're in the right place and need to figure out how to get to that prime position; otherwise, it's probably time for a change.

If you feel like you're in the wrong type of business, have you made that decision solely based on the work and not other factors? We can't help but be swayed by other influences in our lives. The location, the weather, unstable relationships, and a host of other factors could be clouding your view. You can change many of these influences without scrapping a career that you have invested time and talent in and may be the right choice for you. So if you suffer from seasonal affective disorder and need sunshine to be happy, don't work in Sweden in the wintertime or you may hate your job!

Ideally, you want to consider your future options early on. When you're relatively young, hirers are more likely to understand if you started in a different field and now have a better idea of your interests and skills. They realize you will still have time to gain the skills you need for your new career. Older applicants may have a harder time explaining why it took them so long to figure out what they wanted to do for a living and how they will fit into the organization. They are also likely to need higher salaries than younger prospects even if their previous work didn't give them the skills they will need at their new job. An employer might have allocated funds for entry-level workers and not be able to meet an older worker's salary requirements. Lastly, some professionals find it difficult or uncomfortable to manage employees who are much older than themselves and, as a result, would be less likely to hire them.

If you do want to make a change and believe you will need to go to graduate school to prepare yourself for your next career, younger is also better when making that move. You'll be more motivated than you would be if you have family obligations and you won't miss any advancement decisions because of a lack of credentials. Most business schools prefer about three years' working experience for their applicants. At other types of graduate schools, students typically range from just out of college to several years out. You can attend school at night or take time off and go full time. Although there is a money-in/money-out disadvantage of full-time grad school, you would have the advantage of being able to test new fields over summer breaks if you want to change your career.

When you do finally find the profession that you believe will highlight your talents and make you excited about going to work in the morning, it's time to start considering the path ahead of you. Are there many directions you can go from your current job or is it clear that your particular specialty leads to a specific position at your company up the line? Do you want that job or similar ones in the industry in a few years? What job in your industry do you aspire to in five years, 10 years, and 20 years? The best way to figure out the answers to some of these questions is to examine the careers of those ahead of you: the **Experts** and the **Powerhouses.**

Look at the Experts and Powerhouses

You may be nearing the Expert stage at your company or maybe you're just a few years off. Either way, take a look at the career progression of successful colleagues in your industry at various stages ahead of you, from Expert to Powerhouse.

Experts are professionals who manage significant projects and have developed a strong network of internal relationships. Although they don't typically develop strategy, they lead teams that implement the action plans given to them from more senior professionals. As an individual enters the Expert stage, often his job becomes more clearly tied to his company's revenues. He may control budgeting and profitability within a section of his company's business.

An Expert might have responsibility for the firm's clients, lead a group of employees who produce a key product, or manage professionals working in Human Resources. You can enter the Expert, or middle-management stage, of your career anywhere from your mid-20s to 30s, depending on your company and industry. And this transition can occur gradually or through a promotion or internal job change that shifts your role overnight. Smaller entrepreneurial companies tend to present the fastest path to the middle ranks but their employees might be trading advancement speed for the job security and established training programs offered at larger companies. The titles also vary across industries but include customer service manager, district sales manager, plant manager, and accounting manager.

The last career phase, often reached when professionals reach their 40s or 50s, but sometimes earlier, is the Powerhouse stage. Professionals achieve this level only after years of skillful political maneuvering and working to establish their credibility.

Powerhouses have the ability to influence their constituencies, whether those constituencies include senior decision makers at their companies, clients, or both. They are the C-Suite executives, major producers, operating division heads, or **thought leaders**[1] known throughout their industry who shape the direction of company business. Any executive with *Chief* in her title is a Powerhouse. Other typical titles in many organizations for these leaders are partner, national sales manager, general manager, vice president, senior VP, executive VP, executive director, managing director, group president, and president.

Powerhouses have done a lot of things right, including gaining the experiences that have put them in positions of influence in their companies. As you consider the best way to advance in your career, take a look at the backgrounds of the leaders who are in positions you would like to have someday.

But what if you don't know where you want to be in 10 or 20 years? There are so many unknown variables including your social life and family life. How will you prioritize work in the next phase of your career? Will you have children, and, if so, will your family life affect the time you spend at work and your desire to travel? Most women can't predict how they will respond to these questions. Both women who thought they would continue working after they started families, and those who assumed they would stop, have been wrong in their predictions. The reality is you don't know what you will do until you are faced with circumstances that right now are hard to fully appreciate, including enjoying work more than you anticipated.

As Sheryl Sandberg has famously said: "Don't leave before you leave." Sandberg means you should keep your head in the game and plan for career success, not for a career break, or success will not happen. When you suspend any pre-formed notions of how long you will be in the workforce, you will have a much better ability to assess career options.

But even if you assume you will continue working, how can you determine a course if you don't know what career you want at your company? If you don't know, the best strategy is to shoot high. If you were to remain in your company or another in the same industry, what are the top few positions you could imagine yourself reaching in your career? Select a couple that you believe would be interesting and would capitalize on your talents. Then, unless you chose CEO, look at the jobs right above those you picked. Those are the jobs you should put on your radar, the ones you should start to build a skill base for. You don't want to find yourself in a position where your aspirations increase and your experience level hasn't kept up to speed.

Which Skills Do You Need?

You may know you lack the technical abilities and personality skills required for the top spots on your list but experiences and training can change that. Even if you can't fathom a role in the higher-level positions, don't believe you'll be up for the task, or don't want to put in the time to get there, avoid making that decision at the beginning of your career. As you gain experience in your business, you will develop a better understanding of your particular strengths and weaknesses. With frequent self-assessments, you can focus on strengthening your weak spots and capitalizing on your talents. Then you can further define your game plan. Many professionals don't have the proper level of insight early on to pinpoint where they will best fit in an organization. Statistically, men overestimate their talents and women underestimate theirs. That's enough reason to be ambitious at the beginning of your career; you probably have more potential than you realize.

After you target jobs in your company or industry, you need to learn about the work history of the executives who hold those jobs. Talk to the leaders themselves or to colleagues who might be familiar with their careers. You can also look at company websites, LinkedIn, industry news sites, search engines, and, if you are working at a public company, proxy filings. The Securities and Exchange Commission (SEC) requires public companies to file proxy statements before they hold their annual shareholder meetings. These filings give biographical information on the highest-paid executives at each public company. You can often find them in the *Investor Relations* tab on company websites under SEC filings. If it's not listed there, you can search the SEC website under EDGAR[2] filings (SEC Form DEF 14A). Overall, it will be easier to obtain information on your own company's leaders, but it's good to be aware of the differences among companies in your industry.

Review the positions that the leaders held during their careers and then determine the skills they acquired during each of these roles. You can find out this information by talking with colleagues to learn about different jobs within your company. Try to get a sense of the duties people have in each department; you may discover an interesting area that you had never heard of. Sometimes the job title, along with the commensurate job skills, will be obvious to you, but if you dig deeper you'll learn more. And if you can find out about the specific accomplishments of the leaders you've identified, you'll discover even more. If a leader took over a group that had just lost half its members to a competitor, you'll realize he had acquired important crisis management skills that could have contributed to his rise in the company.

Gathering information about the leaders on your list will help you understand the career stops and skill sets that will be helpful for you as you advance at your company. Although especially today, most careers aren't linear and can seem to branch out into areas unrelated to a leader's primary function. Generally these positions will contribute skills, despite the seeming lack of logic in moving from one spot to the next, but not always. Maybe an executive was filling a void where she could be helpful but the position wasn't necessarily career enhancing. Or possibly she was in a temporary position while another critical one opened up. So the more information you can gather about different executives and the closer you get to discussing careers with those who hold the positions you aspire to, the better able you will be to plan your career.

Also try to determine your leaders' experience outside your company. Were most of the senior executives working at your organization for the last several years or were many of them hired from outside? Although remaining at your job tends to be the least disruptive, some organizations and entire industries tend to provide attractive opportunities to those entering from competitor companies. In turn, employees see a transfer as a way to catalyze a career that would advance more slowly if they stayed. The leaders you're viewing probably made wise choices relative to their shifts but it is possible to move too much. Hiring managers fear that a potential employee who has changed companies frequently might do the same at her new company. Recruiters also want to ensure the professional doesn't have a record of underperformance, which would cause the high turnover.

Do the professionals whose careers you are examining all have international experience? If so, does that mean you need to check that box? Analyze their backgrounds further; if they were senior execs when they were sent abroad, you probably don't need to rush for that experience early in your career; you just need to develop the skill set to put you in the running for a job abroad if it does arise. By the way, if you do consider going abroad, make sure you have a way home. Especially if you are a junior employee, your company may have no clear plan for your return and you could get marooned overseas with no openings back at your home country. Take a look at other employees at your same level who have accepted an offer abroad to see what has happened to them.

While you are reviewing others' backgrounds, you may discover you need to take classes or earn a degree to gain skills or credentials for advancement. You can check your own company to see if training is offered internally; if not, consider attending classes outside. Hopefully, your company will be willing to pay for some or all of it, so make sure you ask.

Lastly, if you hope to advance to the executive ranks of your company, take a look at the leaders as a whole to determine the prevalent background. Certain companies and industries tend to have executives with expertise in one prominent area. Leaders in some sectors of the technology industry primarily have software development backgrounds, while heavy industry execs often have manufacturing backgrounds. In my industry, investment banking, virtually everyone has a finance background, but some companies historically drew their top executives from the sales and trading side of the business and others elevated managers from the banking side to the CEO post. So even within an industry, different companies can have their own culture that plays into which types of professionals manage the business.

Knowing as much as you can about how successful industry players have gained experience will help you make your own career decisions. The risk in reviewing the information though is that it's easy to make broad generalizations. Drill down on why and when successful colleagues went in the direction they did by asking them or others who might know. Without finding out the real details you might make an obvious conclusion that isn't true. Also realize that the career progression of someone 20 or 30 years your senior may not reflect changes to your industry impacting which skills will be valued in your company in the future.

Acquiring New Skills

After analyzing leaders at your company and others in your industry, you should have a picture of what skills you will need and what jobs can help you gain those skills. The best scenarios for young professionals are those that identify a few paths to follow. Managers don't always have the ability to promote capable employees. Work hierarchies are pyramid structures that put a strain on the capacity at the top for good people. But some departments may have a greater number of Expert-level positions and therefore more opportunity to move into those slots. Ideally, you want to make sure your background gives you options to move into another area so you're not stuck in a job without upward mobility.

At this point you have talked to a lot of people, investigated senior jobs, and figured out the skills you will need to get to a few different high-level positions in the future. If you can gain more of the skills you need within your department, tell your boss what you've learned and see if he has any other perspectives on skills required to get to your desired position. Then discuss how you can gain that experience in his department. Do you need different types of assignments or different responsibilities? Help your boss to buy into your goals and make him a part of developing your career to achieve them.

If you can't gain any more useful skills at your current job, you may need to move into a different group. The move could be as easy as applying for an internal job posting. But if your company doesn't advertise openings through internal listings, or you want a job that's not available through an inter-office listing, you may need to request help from a mentor or your boss.

If you suspect your boss will be unhappy to lose you, the process could be more delicate. It's almost always best to discuss your desire to move with your boss before you accept a position. The bigger question is, how advanced should your discussions with another group be before you have that conversation? In an ideal world, you would tell your manager that you want to make a move and he would help you facilitate it. Even with excellent employees, many managers realize that the pyramid structure doesn't allow for much upward mobility. An internal change would mean losing a good employee but giving another a chance to move up.

But bosses aren't always so altruistic. If yours is more worried about losing you, the timing of your discussions will be a judgment call on your part. Maybe he lacks a replacement or maybe he will feel offended by your choice. If you're worried about his response, you can nearly lock up another position before you approach him. Then tell him you would like to expand your skill base and ask for his help in making a shift to the other group. It's tricky business and each situation is different. There's no definitive roadmap but you will probably have a sense of how to approach the situation when the time comes.

The job that allows you to build your skill base may be a promotion of sorts or it could be a lateral transfer. Generally lateral transfers to areas where you don't have experience are easier within your own company than outside of it. If you haven't had success moving within, you'll need to go outside your company. And sometimes, the only way to gain the right experience is to join a group inside or outside your organization at a more junior level. Although it may feel like a step backward, you will be positioning yourself for greater advancement in the future.

Armed with all this information on planning your career, you will probably recognize where Ava, an in-house lawyer in an industrial company, went wrong in planning hers.

Ava joined a company in the heavy manufacturing industry and had been working in the in-house legal area since her graduation from law school five years before. She began thinking more seriously about her career after she hit the five-year milestone and started to analyze some of her colleagues' careers. Ava realized that most of the senior executives in her company had gained experience in manufacturing. Law was interesting, but at her company, it wasn't going to carry her career to the top.

As she began to consider the best way to make an internal career shift, a few colleagues transferred out of the legal department. Their departure left a gap, and to her surprise, she was promoted to assistant vice president, the level right below the top position in her group, general counsel. Her department was understaffed and she immediately gained responsibility and began to work on high-profile projects. Ava put her plan to move within the company on hold and decided to focus on her new position. Part of her decision was influenced by a rumor that her boss was planning to retire soon. Ava suspected that if she stayed in the legal department, it wouldn't be long before she might become general counsel.

Ironically, not too long after Ava was promoted, the manufacturing division manager approached her with an opportunity. The manager called it a lateral move but now that she had been promoted, it was a bit of a step back. Ava knew it would be a great way to add to her skill base but it was hard to consider now that she was more senior on the legal staff. Since she also had her eye on her boss's job, she turned down the offer. Ava rationalized that a rapid promotion to general counsel would position her better in her company in the long term.

The department head did retire, but not for five years, and a lawyer from the company's outside legal counsel was brought in to head the group. By that time, Ava decided it didn't make sense to join the manufacturing division because she would have had to start at quite a low level. She decided to stay in the legal department.

By making the series of decisions she made, Ava missed an opportunity to gain the experience that she would need to advance much further at her company. She could replace her new department head in a few years, if he moved elsewhere, but it would be difficult for her to move into a senior line, or producing position, without any experience in that area.

Ava realized later that she could have made a better decision by talking to her boss. He was not the type to feel threatened by junior staff members so she would have felt comfortable asking him if the rumors of his retirement were true. He may have told her, or he may not have, but there would have been no loss in asking. And at the same time, Ava would have been conveying her own ambitions. If she was lucky, her boss would have told her he was planning to retire in five years but she would still be too junior at that point to take over. After that conversation, no doubt Ava would have made a different career move.

NOTE TO FILE:

- Talk, talk, and talk some more to mentors, colleagues, and industry contacts. The more information you have to plan your career, the better.
- Many skill sets allow for many opportunities.

Indispensable Line Experience

Ava needed to acquire critical skills in order to be promotable to the top level of her organization. Those skills are developed through **line** experience. The revenue-generating positions at a company such as those in manufacturing, brand management, and sales make up the line jobs, while revenue-consuming jobs, such as accounting, legal, and personnel management, comprise **staff** jobs. Revenue-generating line positions create pathways to senior positions where employees gain profit and loss (P&L) experience and responsibility. You can also gain that experience early on. For instance, you might start out as a sales assistant and then graduate to a sales representative and have clients of your own. Your manager will likely expect you to budget your own P&L by estimating sales growth, client expansion, and costs. She will take into account your individual projections when she develops the total expected numbers for her team of sales people. That pattern continues up the line until ultimately the CEO is using company-wide numbers to make operational decisions for the company.

When you become a division leader in a line position you will lead a team, make hiring and firing choices, set strategy for your group, and make decisions regarding the product or service you manage. The job is like running a little company, which is why line experience is essential for most top executive jobs. The Wall Street Journal Task Force,[3] charged with advising companies on how to achieve gender parity at senior levels, listed granting P&L leadership to women as its top recommendation.

A great by-product of working in a line job is that your results are easily recognizable and quantifiable. There shouldn't be any confusion by you or your manager in determining how productive you are.

The career of Mary Barra, appointed CEO of General Motors in 2014, shows how line experience set her up to be the board's pick for top leader of the historically male-run car company. Early on she held a variety of administrative and engineering positions and then jumped to the next level of visibility within GM when she was selected to run a manufacturing plant. She also acted as Vice President of Global Manufacturing Engineering, Vice President of Global Human Resources, Vice President of Global Purchasing and Supply Chain, and Executive Vice President of Global Product Development. At 52 years of age, Barra accomplished a lot even before she won the nod for CEO. It helped that the outgoing CEO, Dan Akerson, thought highly of her; it also helped that she had attained a variety of skills, including those in revenue-producing areas of the company. She showed that she could handle the top spot.

NOTE TO FILE:

- There is no more important criterion than *line experience* for most executive-level jobs.

Your Sponsor as Your Co-Pilot

True sponsorship is a special gift in one's career. Sponsors' responsibilities go beyond the typical mentors' duties of giving guidance and advice. A sponsor paves the way for his protégé to land in strategically important roles at his company. He highlights her accomplishments with senior leaders, he gives her crucial training in areas in which she needs help, and he protects her should she misstep along the way.

I am thankful for a sponsor I had early in my career who threw me a lifeline. Chip and I had worked together at two different firms on Wall Street before I left to go to business school. We moved together to the second firm; although we weren't a package deal, Chip had handled the negotiations for both of us. The director of the bank we were joining was eager to hire Chip, who used his leverage to arrange for a step up in title and compensation for me. After I left for school, Chip and I kept in touch, although I changed careers and entered the real-estate industry after graduation.

But soon after I embarked on my new career I realized I wanted to return to banking. I liked the fast-paced environment and the ability to work on deals in a variety of industries. At this point I kept returning to the same thought: It would have been so much easier if I made this realization while I was still in business school and could interview with investment banks there. Still, I started my job search not knowing how difficult the process would be. One of my first interviews was with a banker who I was introduced to through a classmate from business school. The meeting seemed to proceed well until the very end. The banker said I had the right skills for the job but then added: "If you were a true investment banker, you would have a passion . . . a fire in your belly. You would never have left the Street."

My first reaction was surprise that anyone actually said "fire in your belly" in real life. My second was that I was screwed. I had no idea working in real estate for a year would brand me a turncoat. I tried to defend myself but I'm sure my explanation for leaving banking sounded to him like I had defected to North Korea. By the end of our conversation I knew there was no opportunity for me at this bank; I wasn't sure about any others.

Fortunately, my friend Chip offered me a position at the small investment house he had recently joined. Although I left two years later for another opportunity at Merrill Lynch, I am forever grateful for the sponsorship Chip gave me. He led me to new situations, each time negotiating a promotion on my behalf with the hiring managers.

Sylvia Ann Hewlett, author of *Forget a Mentor, Find a Sponsor,*[4] reminds us that sponsorship is a two-way street. Sponsors critically need dependable professionals who can drop into challenging situations and produce quality outcomes. They also might benefit from trusted employees who complement their skill base with a different set of talents. All of these characteristics will increase a sponsor's productivity, performance, and stature at his company. Of course, aside from the impact on their own work, sponsors select employees to support who they respect and genuinely enjoy.

The career highlights of a business school classmate of mine, Jim Weber, show how sponsorship can catapult you to the next level in your career. As four-time president of sports-related companies, his path also demonstrates that gaining line experience, acquiring important skills, and taking on challenging assignments are critical to career success. Jim runs Brooks Running Company, which you probably know as the maker of Brooks running shoes and apparel. He's had lots of bosses before, but right now reports to Warren Buffett, whose company, Berkshire Hathaway, bought Brooks in 2006. Buffett is known for selecting businesses that have exceptional management. As a stockholder of Brooks for many years, Buffett obviously likes what he sees.

After graduating from the University of Minnesota, Jim began work at a commercial bank. "I learned how to tear financial statements apart and to connect them to business strategy and performance," Jim told me. "It was fantastic training that I have used throughout my career." But after getting a handle on how to assess a company's condition, Jim began to think that his firm's clients were having a lot more fun than he was. They made strategic decisions that would mean success or failure for their companies. They could take a small idea and turn it into a powerful brand. Before long, Jim decided to make a career change that would allow him to one day run his own company. He decided to gain skills first by getting an MBA at Dartmouth's Amos Tuck School and upon graduation joined The Pillsbury

Company's Corporate Development division, working on mergers and acquisitions.

At Pillsbury, Jim reported to Jerry Levin who saw potential in his young employee. He recommended Jim for a special assignment, working as assistant to the CEO, where Jim gained exposure to top company leaders. With Jerry's support, Jim then switched into the prepared dough division, the crown jewel of a company known for its identifiable Doughboy. Jim moved into the division to pick up some of the marketing experience that many of the senior executives at his company had acquired. In a company whose revenues depend significantly on the way consumers perceive its products, Jim knew he needed to learn marketing skills. After he gained a foothold in the group, Jerry, who had left Pillsbury to become CEO of The Coleman Company, the outdoor and camping goods provider, asked Jim to join him.

Jim joined The Coleman Company, working on whatever project Jerry saw as the highest priority of the moment. One such priority was to review a money-losing, $15 million in sales division. After taking a look at the unit, Jim told Jerry that it needed a lot of attention and he thought he could fix it. At age 29, having never managed anyone, Jim was taking over a 150-person struggling business at Coleman. He turned that division around successfully and next took over another Coleman unit, O'Brien International, maker of water ski and water sport products.

Jim concedes he has been lucky in his career. He had great sponsorship from Jerry and up to that point hadn't made any bad career decisions. About two months into running his next company, though, he began to wonder if his luck was running out. He helped successfully reposition O'Brien International, which was then for sale, and he made the decision to leave, accepting a job outside of Coleman as President of Sims Sports, a leading marketer in the rapidly growing sport of snowboarding. When Jim took over Sims, the company's business had to be reorganized and repositioned to survive. It's difficult to restructure any company, especially when employees fear changes may threaten their jobs. In the case of Sims, the organization's culture also had to change as it needed to boost quality control by bringing product design and engineering inside and eliminating its licensing programs. But Jim had presided over enough tough transitions that he was confident he could make it work. What he hadn't fully appreciated was a conflicted board of directors with a variety of different agendas, none of which seemed to agree with Jim's growth strategy. After realizing that he and the board were worlds apart on how to manage the company, Jim began to re-think his decision to join Sims. He had to fix the problems he had inherited but was getting no support from above. Recalling how he felt at the time, Jim told me, "I misjudged the partners I had joined. If I could have turned back the clock, I would not have taken that job as it was indeed a mess."

But that mess was probably the best career tutorial Jim ever received. He worked through challenging restructuring problems as well as difficult issues with the board. "I wouldn't call my time at Sims fun, but that experience made me a much better leader. I can draw on the learnings from all the problems thrown at me at Sims." Jim's next CEO role was at Brooks, also struggling with losses and a failing strategy. Jim has tightened the company's focus from a shoe that served too many markets to one that focuses on runners, an adjustment that increased profitability. His changes also improved workplace morale and loyalty and gained Brooks a spot on Outside Magazine*'s list of "Best Places to Work" for the last three years. With a thriving company and a content shareholder in Buffett, Jim doesn't see any need to move on from Brooks any time soon. As CEO of a company that holds Friday theme runs and whose motto is "Run Happy," why would he?*

Jim's experiences are great examples of the benefits of sponsorship and taking on challenging line assignments to gain the skills needed to lead. Building experience in finance and marketing was particularly helpful for a CEO of a variety of consumer sports companies.

Although the skills required for each industry vary, Heidrick & Struggles, an executive search and leadership consulting firm, lets us take a look at the backgrounds of the CEOs for the largest companies in the world.

A few years ago, Heidrick & Struggles conducted a study analyzing the careers of all the existing Fortune 500 CEOs at the time. As the company reported in *Forbes*[5] magazine, more CEOs started their career in finance than any other area, totaling 30% of all of the leaders. The next most prevalent field for these CEOs to have begun their career in was sales and marketing, which captured 20% of the group. Not surprisingly, most of the CEOs were appointed from the position of President or COO. The research further revealed that while more than 75% of the top leaders were appointed internally, less than a third had been at their company most of their careers. And nearly half of the CEOs served on public company boards outside of their own organizations before being named chief executive of the Fortune 500 companies they led.

Jeffrey S. Sanders, Vice Chairman, Heidrick & Struggles[6] and author of the article, noted that "While this portrait of a CEO could shift in the coming years, most of the attributes reflected in our findings are likely to become only more pronounced with the passage of time: financial acumen will continue to be important in an increasingly globalized and economically interdependent world, companies will place a high value on organizational and cultural knowledge, and an increasing number of executives will look to board service as a way of gaining a broader perspective prior to becoming CEO."

The trend toward outside board membership as a stepping-stone to the CEO spot could be a benefit to women. Boards are under scrutiny by investors, public interest groups, and Tweeters alike to increase their number of female non-executive board members. Twitter was shamed into adding its first female board member prior to its initial public offering recently due to public outcry on Twitter, among other places.

Board, C-suite, or CEO selection are all possibilities for you. But first, plan to acquire the necessary skills dictated by the industry you are in, including critical P&L experience. You should also frequently reassess your career goals and your achievements to make sure you are on track for success. Every year isn't too often and can help you fine-tune areas of your professional growth.

NOTE TO FILE: 

- CEOs are often selected based on their line experience accomplishments.
- Women hold[7] 41% of board seats in Norway and 17% in the United States.

Chapter 4: Relationship Building

"Why did you do all this for me?" he asked. "I don't deserve it. I've never done anything for you."

"You have been my friend," replied Charlotte. "That in itself is a tremendous thing."

—Charlotte and Wilbur, *Charlotte's Web*

Will was a young associate at a leading law firm when he got a call from Taylor. Earlier in the week, he and Taylor, also an associate, split up the project work they were assigned and planned to piece together both sides that afternoon. Will didn't care which part of the assignment he had to work on, so he let Taylor pick. In fact, he let Taylor call most of the shots whenever they worked together. Taylor's persuasiveness left Will dumbstruck. Will told me, "He could convince me to do twice as much work as him and I would have thanked him for it."

When the call came in that morning, Will noticed it was from a line outside the office.

"Hi Will, it's Taylor."

"Hey dude, where are you?"

"Oh, I'm home. I wanted to really dig deep into this project without any interruptions. Hey, I was thinking . . . why don't the two of us get together and bounce some ideas around about the assignment?"

"Well, yeah," Will replied, "isn't that what we're doing this afternoon?"

"Oh sure, but I mean before that. We can talk about the case law."

Will understood. Taylor needed help. "No problem, just grab me when you get here," he responded.

The line was silent for a second then Taylor replied, "You know, I think sometimes these things are good to focus on offsite. Then we can really brainstorm. Why don't you come to my place?"

Before he knew it, Will was in a subway heading up to Taylor's apartment.

Taylor didn't know how to approach the work and needed Will's help but didn't want to be caught in the office getting a tutorial on some fairly basic stuff. "Taylor was bright," Will told me, "but he was more of a visionary than a nuts-and-bolts kind of guy. He was very good at leveraging people to gain success."

As it turns out, a few guys other than Will must have been influenced by Taylor's relationship skills. He honed them even further and went on to become managing partner of one of the leading law firms in the United States.

As Taylor would no doubt agree, relationship building is one of the most critical activities you can pursue to develop a successful career. ***Networking,*** *or* ***relationship building,*** *is a process used to develop long-term relationships with others for mutual benefit. Whatever you call it, you have to work on developing connections with colleagues and business associates in order to have a successful career.*

If you don't have an innate ability to easily develop relationships, don't worry, you're not alone. Very few professionals, even those we consider extroverts, effortlessly connect with everyone. Most have to make an effort to network, but the effort usually pays off. Psychologists have discovered that the more familiar a person is with another, the more they tend to like them. This *familiarity principle*[1] helps us in the office. All you need to do is to help people to get to know you.

Broaden Your Network

Most professionals know they should strengthen relationships with senior managers, but many don't realize that cultivating friendships with same-level colleagues, or those junior to them, is important too. If your associate in the next cubicle has become one of your best friends, you will happily spend time with her. But how about that quiet guy who is tough to talk to? Or what about your junior colleague? In the office, it's easy to hang with the people who fit in with you socially, but it's worth the effort to get to know others as well. Colleagues will appreciate your attempts to be friendly, especially those outside of your normal circle.

There are several groups of people who are worth getting to know at the office. If you do, you'll not only help your career, but you'll also enjoy working more. You're spending a third of your life at work, so you might as well have fun!

Administrative Assistants. Admins are the backbone of an organization. They make sure everything runs smoothly and you get to where you need to be when you need to be there. Despite the essential work they do, assistants have pretty lousy jobs sometimes. There are always a few professionals who don't treat them with respect. What these people don't realize is that admins do hold a fair amount of power. They are in charge of their workflow and can prioritize the requests upon them as they see fit. Assistants can also help you gain access to senior professionals. If you need to set up a meeting or get a letter signed, all of your requests go through your colleague's gatekeeper.

Admins also tend to know more about what's going on in the office than do others, and not just who's sleeping with who (interesting—but that's not the focus here). Assistants often have access to information about organizational shifts, project assignments, client interactions, and pay decisions. Some talk, some don't. But like anyone, assistants are more likely to reveal information to those whom they like. Next time you're running out for coffee, remember your admin. She would probably like a cup too.

Subordinates. Your subordinates are an essential part of your team who may directly or indirectly affect your performance. You will be best served if the junior professionals enjoy working for you. That doesn't mean you have to be easy on them; it means you have to respect them and understand their other work-related responsibilities. Who knows, your first-year trainee may end up being your client one day . . . or even your boss.

Once, when I interviewed for a job, I discovered just how influential junior colleagues can be. The prospective hirer noticed where I had previously worked and said, "Oh, you must know John Doe." And I replied, "Of course, I worked with John Doe." We proceeded to have a great conversation, so I assumed I nailed the interview. But I found out the following week from a friend at the hiring firm that I had been blackballed by John Doe. This former colleague of mine had a reputation for working well with senior colleagues but treated everyone under him, especially the support staff, horribly. After giving him a few warnings about his behavior, I told him his bonus would decline because of his treatment of the office personnel. He was furious. I guess he settled the score.

I wouldn't have changed my previous management of my colleague, but it did open my eyes to the power that each person holds in the office, even those junior to me.

Support Personnel. This group is critical when you need office support such as technical help; there's often a long line for their services.

In my first job when I took my work into the department that produced the client presentation books, it seemed forever before I got my books back. I tried connecting with the production manager, but she sort of scared me. She never smiled or would acknowledge that she heard me when I told her my deadline. But a couple of my colleagues thought she was nice and easy to deal with. I was trying to figure out why she didn't like me when one of the guys I worked with told me "she always schedules the men's work first." I initially felt relieved that I hadn't done something to alienate her, but then I became annoyed. Eventually I realized, if you can't beat 'em . . . so whenever I needed a rush job I gave it to one of my male colleagues to take in. I wasn't able to develop a relationship with the production manager, but I did the next best thing—I connected with others who could help.

Peers. Your peers are often your closest friends at the company. They will be great connections if either one of you move departments or companies, so keep in touch with them no matter where they go. Also branch out to peers in other divisions as much as you can.

Your Direct Superior. The person who determines your project selection, suitability for promotion, and pay requires a lot of attention. She will also likely understand your strengths and weaknesses and you can learn from her. If you respond to her advice and suggestions and develop a strong relationship with her, she could also help make introductions for you to other senior officers in your company.

Any Other Superior. Try to develop relationships with other superiors in your group as well as those outside of it. The more senior you are at your company, the more influence executives across the organization will have on your career. High-level appointments and promotions often involve the input from executives in a number of different areas.

Clients. A strong relationship will stack the odds in your favor when your client puts new business out for bid. Even among very senior professionals, clients generally voice their approval or disapproval of the job to their account representative's superior. If you don't have external clients, you probably have *internal clients* at your company who are relying on your services to complete your job. An example of an internal client would be a product manager to an internal package designer. The designer may work in a separate Design Engineering department but supports the product through the manager's requests. Those types of internal clients are also important to your advancement.

Spouses/Partners of Colleagues and Clients. It's surprising how much influence they can have. When you see them in the office or socially, take time to have a conversation.

Whether you have mentors, industry contacts, or simply friends outside of your company, they can all be helpful during discussions regarding your career. They're also good touch points in the event you consider leaving your job and need to look for another.

NOTE TO FILE: 

- Respect and appreciate everyone you work with, junior or senior.

How Do You Network?

In the early 1930s, Dale Carnegie, the same man who created the classes that Warren Buffett credits with changing his life, wrote a book titled *How to Win Friends and Influence People*. The book, which has sold 15 million copies, gave instruction on making friends, having an impact, being a leader, reducing stress, and enjoying life. Some of his principle teachings are the basis of networking.

Carnegie's Tips

Carnegie says that people are more receptive to those who smile, seem positive, and don't criticize. The simple gesture of smiling has a tremendous effect on others. It enhances first impressions, reduces conflict, and increases the likelihood of better personal and professional relationships.

Andrew Kindfuller, currently CEO of ScentAir and formerly COO of Guthy-Renker International, the company that markets Proactiv Solution, told me how smiling influenced which celebrity Proactiv chose for its spokesperson. "Guthy conducted focus groups with several different actors and singers and noticed the viewers responded more favorably to celebrities who smiled the most. That's why we selected Jessica Simpson as one of our first spokespeople. She became a breakthrough endorser."

Smiling and being generally positive have the same effect on co-workers. Their presence makes work more enjoyable. Studies have also shown that people trust and are more willing to make friends with others who have a positive outlook on life.

Focusing your attention on the other person is another tip Dale Carnegie says will help you connect with others. Address the person by name, talk about his interests, and sincerely make him feel important. Using the person's name in a conversation might not come naturally but it has a big impact. You can probably think of people you know who sprinkle your name throughout the conversation; it's seductive.

In middle school, a group of my friends and I all wanted to date the same boy. He didn't talk much and none of us thought he was particularly cute or cool. But unlike the other boys, when he said hello in the hall, he called us each by name. I realize it doesn't take much for a bunch of 8th-grade girls to develop a crush, but if he didn't use our names, we probably would never have noticed him.

We all like to hear compliments. While you may bond with some of your closest friends through ragging on each other, at some point you've told them they made the right choice, or did a good job, and they've told you the same. Sincere compliments can build trust and friendship between co-workers as well.

Carnegie also believed that being a good listener and discussing other people's interests will help you connect with people. Today he would probably include giving the speaker your undivided attention and not glancing down at your phone. Everyone wants to know they are interesting to others. You can demonstrate your desire to find out more about someone by asking them about themselves and their hobbies. Even if your new contact seems completely different from you, if you delve deep enough, you'll probably find some similarities that will help you along with your conversation.

Though Dale Carnegie's principles are still relevant today, successful professionals need to go beyond connecting and strive to bond with colleagues. The trust and loyalty of a close colleague can give you insights, warn you of pitfalls, and guide you throughout your career. Whether you bond with a sponsor, mentor, peer, or subordinate, each has talents to offer you and you to them. And the more invested you are in a professional relationship, the more likely your co-worker and you will pull together to come up with the right solution for both of you.

You Gotta Be You

Whatever strategies you follow to develop strong professional relationships, one requirement is more important than all others: you need to be yourself. Yes, you may be on the edge of your comfort zone trying to connect with people but you shouldn't try to act like a world-class salesperson if that's just not your style. If you're quiet and clumsy, don't worry; your colleague may find you endearing and funny. Trying to be anything else will feel false to you and come off as disingenuous to others.

You may be wondering how your genuine personality will add value to a relationship. It's easy to look at a senior officer and question why she would want to waste time developing a relationship with you. If that's how you feel, you're not focusing on the talents you have to offer. Execs like hearing junior employees' perspectives and can easily learn from the next generation. There's a good chance that you know more about technology and social media trends than your senior colleagues, and if you come from a different part of the country or worked in a different industry, you offer a perspective that others don't have.

One of my college friends, Cassie, didn't feel comfortable making conversation with senior management. She knew she had an unhealthy respect, or was it fear, of company executives and wasn't sure how that would change. But the spring after she joined her company, a conversation about baseball at the end of a meeting turned her perspective around.

Cassie understood more about baseball than anyone I knew, including my male friends who seemed to do nothing but follow sports. She admitted to being a little obsessed. Cassie analyzed teams and players and could recall statistics, league history, and specific plays.

At the end of the particular meeting at work, talk turned to baseball and a senior colleague forecast that the Braves were going to win the National League. That's all Cassie had to hear, and without thinking, she looked at the senior officer and blurted out: "That will never happen." When she heard the word "baseball," the section of her brain that controls judgment shut down. At that point Cassie said she immediately felt the temperature in the room rise and sweat began to stream down her back. She knew she had to apologize, but she wasn't sure if sound would come out of her mouth. Opening her mouth at all could be a risk as her stomach muscles were beginning to constrict.

Cassie then remembers seeing the executive gaze at her as if he didn't know she worked at the company. After an uncomfortable few seconds, in a voice much kinder than she deserved, he asked her why she didn't think Atlanta would win. Cassie relaxed slightly after hearing this man ask the question as if he legitimately cared about her answer. She began to give her theory on the St. Louis Cardinals' edge over the Braves in the upcoming series. The conversation lasted longer than any Cassie had had with any senior officer at her company and was the first of many baseball talks the two would have. As the season progressed (and the Cardinals won), the executive became a mentor of Cassie's, all initiated by revealing a knowledge she didn't realize would be valuable in the office.

If you don't have impressive sports knowledge, don't worry, there are plenty of other talents you can offer. Maybe you have tried all of the Thai restaurants in town and can recommend the best. Or you have a better-than-working knowledge of John Adams' and Thomas Jefferson's leadership styles. As a Denver native, can you recommend the ski resorts that locals prefer? Or are you knowledgeable about current events and can offer a perspective on world news?

That last ability is one that every professional should develop. Interest in our world grows as we mature. Most mid-level professionals will tell you they have a greater interest in a broad array of daily news than they did when they were recent graduates. If you don't have that passion yet, it would be helpful to try to develop it. Being able to talk, and have an opinion, on socioeconomic and political events worldwide will help you converse with senior colleagues and gain their respect. At the very least, read the first page of a daily newspaper or news website's front and business sections and the headlines of the city section and the sports page. You can also have alerts sent to your phone by news services or Twitter. One popular service that not only gives you a thumbnail of world events, but explains it to you, is theSkimm.[2] It was started by two women in their 20s who both worked as producers for NBC News; their motto: *We read, you skimm.*

NOTE TO FILE:

- If you can't think of what to talk about, discuss your colleague's favorite subject: him.

Places to Network

Sometimes getting the opportunity to bond is harder than figuring out how to bond. You should take advantage of internal meetings, conferences, training sessions, and work gatherings, which are all great venues for broadening your network. These sessions may come to you as mandatory on-going education requirements or you may have to seek them out. Selecting a training session that will help you acquire the skills you need can also serve the purpose of exposing you to other people in your company. You can even be strategic about the types of courses, picking ones that you need but that also allow you to meet a certain level colleague or one from a specific department. Brief work gatherings will give you other chances to meet more of your co-workers. Go to the 15-minute party in the conference room for an associate's birthday, even if you're busy with a project.

In all of these cases, your focus must be on developing relationships. If you attend a conference and just stick close to your cubicle mates, you won't be helping your career. If you set manageable networking goals you will be successful. Those goals will be different for everyone, but should be achievable and allow you to realize the progress you've made. You might promise yourself that you'll make one good new connection at your company's offsite, or that you'll start a conversation this week with the colleague you always see from the other department.

Industry conferences provide great resources for meeting important connections. Although colleagues in your field might not seem relevant to your career at the time you meet them, they may be helpful for future business transactions and job searches, or to give external perspective on your career questions. At each event, like the internal ones previously referenced, try to stretch a little and talk to someone who is on your radar as they could become a possible mentor or helpful connection.

Occasionally, external meetings offer golf rounds between sessions. Not a golfer myself, I didn't participate in these opportunities and regret never having learned to play. Golf is one of the rare opportunities to hold captive a client or colleague for four hours. Those who don't have the ability to participate lose, at the very least, a chance to get to know their business associate and, at the most, a business deal or career opportunity. If you can possibly learn to play, it will help you in the long run. You don't need to be good; etiquette is more important. If you are delaying fellow golfers, just pick up your ball and take the highest score you can for that hole, which in most circles is three over par. Advance to the next hole and keep chatting.

For many, meeting colleagues for drinks or dinner will be easier and more comfortable than golfing with them. Socializing with your associates after work has become a staple of corporate networking. These gatherings are ideal opportunities to get to know a colleague away from the office when she is a little more relaxed. Lunches work well, too, as do coffee meet-ups. As long as you get your work done on time, you should take advantage of as many team gatherings as you can. If senior colleagues are present, you should especially try to attend. And once again, make sure you talk to the senior people, not just your immediate colleagues.

When I was a junior employee I sometimes went to dinner with senior colleagues who were also in the office late. Dinner was often out of my price range, but I tried to think of my expenditure as an investment in the future. It was rare to be able to spend time with a senior manager out of the office, so I figured the splurge was worth it. If you are in the same situation and your colleague offers to pay, it's probably because she remembers what those first paychecks were like. Accepting a senior manager's offer in that situation is not at all unusual.

You're likely to know you should network when you are in these work-related situations but some great opportunities can also result from being in places that have nothing to do with work. If you're out with your friends and meet someone in your industry or in another that interests you, then that's a relationship you want to develop. Most people will be happy to help if you tell them you would love to learn more about their career. Meeting for coffee has become one of the most commonly accepted networking practices. It doesn't take long, either party can leave at any time if they need to, and it's not intimate; perfect for getting to know a professional contact.

When to Network

I'm always surprised when I offer someone a perfect opportunity to connect and they don't take the bait. I recently met Caroline, a health-care consultant, at a networking event. She worked for a company based in San Francisco that had just merged with another, causing her work group to change. Caroline was newly married; her husband worked in Los Angeles and lived in his parents' house there. While both were willing to move to the other spouse's city, no opportunities had turned up yet for either. That arrangement struck me as dismal for two newlyweds in their 20s. I told her I would be happy to introduce her to a friend who runs the health-care practice at a large Los Angeles–based consulting company. "She may even be hiring," I said, "but if not, she'll at least have some great advice for you."

Caroline's response: "I really do like my new colleagues; I'm just not sure about my new position."

Huh? That was a bit of a disconnect. We kept talking and I offered to connect Caroline again. Again she didn't pick up on my offer. Perhaps she and her new husband liked living apart?

More likely, Caroline didn't feel comfortable leaving her new job just then. Maybe she wanted to make sure she could get good references or she wanted to get a promotion first. But I still couldn't believe she wouldn't jump at the chance to meet a senior woman in health-care consulting, especially one based in the town where her husband lives.

What Caroline didn't understand is that networking is a long-term game. It's unlikely that a casual contact would lead to a direct and immediate benefit, but developing and renewing those contacts will ultimately help you in your career. Caroline needs to develop her industry contacts now for opportunities later. The time that most professionals push their networking efforts into high gear is when they begin a job search. But that's the toughest time to begin to develop relationships because your ultimate goal is obvious and one-sided. If you connect with industry professionals before you need their help, they will be more likely to come through when you are ready to make a career move. Caroline should have met with my friend and kept a dialogue going until she was ready to take the next step. Had she done that, she would have developed a rapport with my contact and might have been able to get support when she needed it the most.

Organizing Your Network

As you become focused on developing your relationships, you may need to create a system to keep track of your network. I heard of one young professional who took organizing his networking activities to a new level. He created an Excel spreadsheet that recorded all of his contacts inside and outside his company, including information on how he met them and any personal and business details such as "he coaches daughter's preschool soccer team" or "husband's name Wes" or "knows Kate Carter from work at Pepsi." He then indicated the date of the last time they were in touch and the circumstances, such as "Starbucks coffee" or "Tampa Beverage Industry Convention." He added a column for the date he planned to contact them again and sorted each person's information by that "next contact" date. So the top of his spreadsheet had the people he needed to contact in order of proposed date to make sure no one fell through the cracks. You're probably not surprised that he entered the names and their "next contact" date into his calendar with pop-up reminders to tell him when to e-mail or call. The process helped him evaluate who he was spending his time on and to determine whether he needed to reprioritize.

Although the spreadsheet approach may seem like overkill, you have to admire the guy for his anal retentiveness. If you can be half as organized as him you should be off to a great start. But make sure you don't let your list drive your actions; consider how to develop your relationship with each person and what kind of relationship you're hoping to achieve. You can't have 20 significant mentor relationships—there's just not enough time. Focus your energies on forging a few close senior and peer relationships, then cultivate a second layer of business contacts that you expect to grow stronger over time.

The type of relationship you are developing will dictate the amount of time you need to spend connecting. You might want to contact a peer in your industry who you see as a long-term career friend every one to four months. For an executive at a competitor company, you might touch base every six months or so.

After you connect, send an e-mail to say you enjoyed meeting and hope to keep in touch. Make sure though that you follow up immediately and don't forget to reference something from your meeting to let her know that you were interested in the conversation. You can also e-mail later with an article that's relevant to your contact. Or you can just send a comment on a recent development. At some point you might want to ask if you can stop by her office (which may be the most convenient for her) or meet for coffee or a drink. Managers are generally happy to help younger professionals, especially if they would like career guidance. If she can't find time, ask if you can give her a call for a few minutes of her advice. All of this interaction could be spread out over a year.

If your contact is within your company, you have a little more latitude. Drop by her office, plan to meet for lunch, call her for advice, or just show up at company events that you know she will attend. If it's someone you know well, perhaps from an earlier project, schedule a once-a-month or once-a-quarter lunch to catch up. Just don't let a solid relationship slide because of neglect.

NOTE TO FILE: 

- Ask yourself each week what new effort you've made to connect.
- Having lunch with a colleague means you're smart, not a slacker.

The Relationship with Your Manager

A few of my friends played on a men's town hockey team that got together once a week. Anyone could join the team so the players ranged from barely able to skate to experienced. One day my friend Steve started talking about the team.

"You know Jeff, right? He's a good player, but he keeps throwing the puck away, passing it to this guy Patrick who can't shoot."

"Steve," I said. "Didn't you know Jeff works for Patrick?"

Steve thought for a moment and then responded, "I wish he worked for me."

Showing support for your boss is a smart career strategy, even if you have to pass him a puck to do so. Ideally, you and your manager will support each other, and you will provide him with the back-up necessary for him to develop his business. He in turn will assist you in gaining the skills you need to grow in your role and could develop into your mentor. Regardless of your ultimate relationship with your manager, initially he will be the person who assigns you projects, writes your reviews, and has a significant impact on your promotion and pay. That relationship is worth spending extra time on to determine what will work best for the two of you.

Get Inside Your Boss's Head

Whether you interact comfortably with your boss or feel awkward when you try to talk to her, it's worthwhile to work on your relationship. One trick I use to try to understand people better is to replay conversations pretending I'm them. After you meet with your boss, review your conversations, but take her perspective. Also assume her responsibilities and imagine the demands and stresses she faces. Go ahead and reiterate her words and you might be able to read more meaning into your conversation. Now listen to your responses as if you were her. How is she viewing your end of the conversation? It's so easy to be completely focused on your own concerns, position, and experiences that you can miss key meanings in conversations. Sometimes you realize that other influences are shaping the way your boss has to carry out her job. That realization might help you gain greater acceptance of her perspective.

Another way to help you work effectively with your manager is to figure out what she values in an employee. For instance, she might particularly value someone who can work independently and hand in finished material without much assistance. In that case, you'll know to draw on your colleagues when you have questions. Or, she might want the final product looking a specific way and doesn't mind if you ask her several questions to ensure it's in the right form. Maybe she likes you to report on your progress or maybe she would rather hear about it when you are finished. Think about your boss's style and the characteristics she appreciates in her subordinates. You can emphasize certain of your own qualities if you know those are ones your boss seeks in a subordinate.

Dealing with Manager Relationship Problems

Some of the most significant boss/subordinate areas of friction arise from the level of responsibility the boss gives to the subordinate. Typically, from the subordinate's viewpoint, more responsibility is better. Some officers are micromanagers, though, and don't feel comfortable letting their employees run with projects independently. If you find yourself in that position, make sure it's your boss's style creating the problem and not his view of your shortcomings. Ask for feedback and take any suggestions he offers. Some managers have a hard time delegating though, no matter how fabulous their team is; that's one occupational hazard which is hard to overcome.

Another situation that can be tricky to deal with is the manager who feels threatened by you. Kathryn Streator, co-founder of Noosphere Marketing, once worked for a manager who seemed threatened soon after she joined his group. Initially he just ribbed her about her education; then his references became more critical. "Didn't they teach you that at Brown?" or, "I thought MBAs knew that kind of thing." Kathryn concluded that her boss felt insecure about his education and her presence was a daily reminder of his insecurities.

As her manager's behavior became increasingly malicious, she began to spend much of her day trying to fix the relationship. Kathryn asked what she could do to help him and offered to do extra work on his projects. When her efforts didn't change her boss's behavior she asked him point blank if there was something she could do to help their rapport. He said he didn't know what she was talking about. Kathryn recalled how she felt during this part of her career, "I woke up with clenched fists every morning. I had to get up half an hour early just to de-stress." The company Kathryn worked for was small. Although she had developed good relationships with other managers in the company, there was nowhere else she could move, so she decided to leave.

If you ever have a manager like Kathryn had, you'd be wise to follow her approach. She made an extra effort to please her boss, she tried to discuss their relationship, and she developed alliances with other managers in the organization. It's less disruptive to fix a problem or to move within your company if you can. If not, you may find that it's best to leave.

Keep Your Manager Informed

Hopefully you will have a great boss: one who will help you gain visibility within your company, place you in situations that highlight your strengths, and help you improve. Part of your manager's job description includes developing his employees so these are all responsibilities that he should be fulfilling. But he might not focus enough on the development side of his job. Or, he simply might have trouble being on top of the performance of all his direct reports. These situations are the norm in the workplace, which is why it's critical that you keep your boss informed about your work. One of the biggest career mistakes a professional can make is assuming his manager understands his accomplishments when he doesn't. Reviews, promotions, and compensation can all suffer as a result.

The easiest way to ensure your manager is up to date is to interact with him often. You can set up meetings to brief him on your achievements and get together casually. Even when you don't have anything specific to report, the more often you have contact with your manager, the better. Try to talk to him whenever you can, even if it's to discuss rain in the forecast. If either of you travel often, find a reason to talk by phone every couple days. E-mail is fine, but you need to actually speak with your boss to really develop your relationship. Either stop by his office or catch up to him as he's walking to a meeting to discuss your project. Suggest having lunch or coffee every once in a while. If possible, meet with your boss out of his office, away from his landline, so that you can have more of his attention. He may not take the initiative to meet with you, but it's your career so you need to be responsible for it.

In your discussions with your manager, let him know what you're doing and the obstacles you have overcome. Corporate leaders often observe that women don't own their achievements. Making your boss aware of your past accomplishments is the best form of self-promotion. Give factual accounts and describe your role. If you're on a project which had obstacles that you resolved, tell your boss about them. Otherwise, he won't know about the problem or the creativity you employed when you hand over the project. Another way to inform your manager is to ask him for input on your solution. His answer will give you guidance and also let him know that you thought through the problem effectively.

On the whole, senior executives don't want to know how *long* you have worked; they want to know how *good* your work is. Sometimes, though, managers don't understand what's involved in the assignment.

I once worked for a manager who assigned my team a set of financial scenarios for a client presentation. Developing the spreadsheet took some time, which my manager understood. But when we presented it to him, it didn't show him what he wanted so he asked us to change it and bring it back that afternoon. My manager was a banker who started his finance career in the pre-Excel spreadsheet era and only had a general appreciation of what the program could do. He also didn't realize he was asking us to scrap the work we did and create a new structure. When I told him we would need another eight hours to rework the material, my boss looked surprised and said, "Don't you just have to push a button?" Telling your boss how long you worked on each project will sound like whining, but making him aware of reasonable time expectations will benefit both of you.

Like any relationship, communication is the lynchpin of success in your rapport with your boss. You need to understand the influences contributing to his requests as well as his expectations. In turn, he needs to know the challenges you overcame on your path to fulfilling his expectations.

NOTE TO FILE:

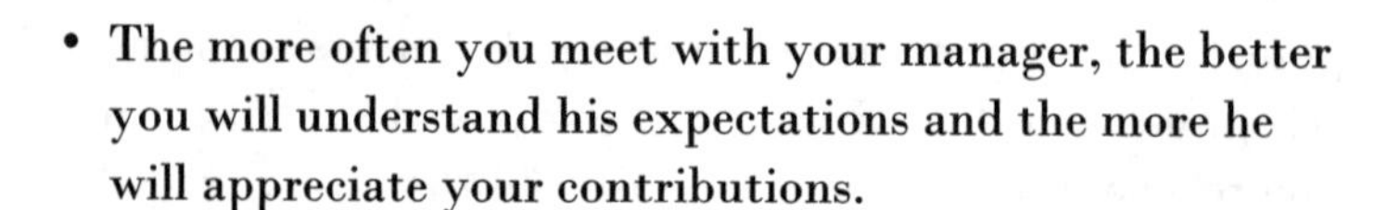

- The more often you meet with your manager, the better you will understand his expectations and the more he will appreciate your contributions.

Developing a Mentor

The best bosses of course turn into mentors. Mentors are trusted advisors who help you with career decisions and advise you on steps to take to advance your career. You can talk easily with mentors, and they make your career journey smoother. Managers can be mentors, but you don't have to have a reporting relationship to take advantage of the benefits of a mentoring connection. You could develop a rapport with someone you've worked with on a project or even someone not in your industry. You can have several mentors who bring you diverse perspectives.

A current boss may have useful insights on alliances within your company and understand the best way to navigate internal politics. A former boss may provide advice on progressing in the industry at large. All of them will have accrued work experiences and gained knowledge of career success factors that they can lend. And a true mentor will know you well enough that his advice encourages you to capitalize on your talents and overcome your weaknesses. Simply having a mentor will make your work more enjoyable. Everyone likes a champion to cheer them on, and when that cheerleader is an accomplished business professional, all the better.

All of these benefits were documented in a study[3] on mentoring over a five-year period with 1,000 Sun Microsystems employees. The researchers found that on average, workers who enrolled in their mentoring program experienced higher pay increases, were promoted five times more often, and stayed employed at the company 72% more than those mentees not participating in the program.

Yet nearly one in five professional women don't have mentors, according to a LinkedIn study[4]. More than half of those who didn't said that "they never encountered someone appropriate." But finding a good mentor isn't a matter of merely *encountering* one. You have to put forth an effort to get to know a colleague and afford them the opportunity to get to know you. Your company may offer a mentoring program, but even if you participate in it, you should continue to forge relationships with other senior officers. Mentors may move and become less accessible, making other mentor relationships that much more important. And sometimes mentors have their own special abilities; while one may be perfect to answer certain questions, another might be better for other types of dilemmas.

How to Acquire a Mentor

So how exactly do you obtain a mentor? *Mentor* is just a word that institutionalizes a relationship. You need the relationship first so don't ever ask anyone to be a mentor. That would be like asking someone to fall in love with you. A potential mentor is either going to want to continue spending time to help you with your career or not. Her interest in advising you will be a function of her impression of your potential, the depth of your relationship, and possibly what you can offer her in return. If you make her laugh, remind her of her younger self, or make her feel charitable as a result of her mentoring, then she's more inclined to want to act as your advisor.

Mentors can gain tangible benefits from their mentees as well. The Sun Microsystems study mentioned earlier also analyzed the impact of mentoring on senior professionals' careers. Mentors, on average, experienced pay increases, were promoted six times more often, and stayed at the company 69% more than those who didn't mentor. The Sun Microsystems data reflect trends that prevail in other well-managed organizations. Those professionals who mentor young people, assist in recruiting, and are perceived to add to their organization in a selfless way, tend to be more successful than those who aren't team players.

Mentoring can also expand a senior's sphere of influence, gaining him more clout within his office. A successful professional, such as Jim Weber, mentee to mentor Jerry Levin at Pillsbury and Coleman, can produce better results for the company, which will reflect well on a mentor, whether they are in the same department or not. Jim said he was known as "Jerry's guy" in both organizations. Junior employees also bring specialized knowledge to a relationship that older professionals may not have and allow their seniors to better understand the generation of workers below them who they need to motivate and lead.

Sometimes, without much effort on anyone's part, mentors just happen. Often a superior and his direct report develop a great rapport that turns into a mentoring relationship. If you have identified people who you believe would be great advisors, but you don't come in contact with them much, you will need to use your networking skills to develop the relationship. It's easy to connect with a potential mentor by asking for advice or feedback. Just ensure you are asking legitimate questions that also show you have put a great deal of thought into the issue. It's best to get to know a potential mentor by discussing business issues before you jump into career questions. Then the senior manager can get a sense of the way you think and how you respond to business dilemmas. These conversations are all a part of developing a bond based on shared values and respect between the two of you. Your job is to be yourself and be diligent about building the relationship. Then you will turn the corner into a comfortable rapport that feels more and more like a close friendship in which both individuals want to see the other succeed.

Mentors Give Advice, You Make Decisions

Once you have developed that type of relationship, make sure you evaluate the advice you are given and don't simply take it as doctrine. Mentors, like everyone else, arrive at decisions with different influences affecting them. A mentor who is your boss might recommend a course of action to keep you working with her. Following her advice may truly be the best choice, but keep in mind her motivations.

A mentor's background also plays a role in forming her recommendations. Did she have a bad experience or a boss she disliked in her career? That history could make your advisor savvy regarding potential difficulties for you, but it could also make her biased against a specific path.

Lastly, it's important to remember that mentors aren't always right. We tend to select our advisors because of their strong character traits and patterns of success. And some of us elevate mentors to superhero status. But no office professional is infallible, especially when it comes to predicting the future.

You need to make the final decision regarding important career choices. Consider all of the alternatives available to you, not just the ones selected by your advisor. Analyze the downside risks, as well as the upside, and think about next steps should downside scenarios play out. If your mentor thinks you should take an opportunity offered in another division, consider the paths you can take from there. You know that position will build your skill base but what happens next? You may notice that the division is top heavy with managers just above your level. Where can you advance from there? If you don't move up as fast as you expect, will you stay or seek another transfer? You can't possibly know the answers to the questions, but thinking through scenarios with or without mentors will best prepare you for possible career decisions in your future.

NOTE TO FILE: 

- Listen to many advisors, and then make your decision.

The Sponsor Relationship

While a mentor will lend advice and suggestions, sponsors go one step further. Sponsors are senior managers willing to advocate for you, help you gain visibility, and cultivate new senior relationships. They understand that promotions and high-quality assignments often come from being well-known throughout the company, and they look for opportunities to create that exposure. They recommend you for great projects or make sure you are invited to join task forces or committees. True sponsors help their protégés, even if they work in different areas of the company.

Women, especially, need sponsors to help them navigate a path to the top. Sylvia Ann Hewlett, Chairman and CEO of the Center for Talent Innovation,[5] conducted research on women in the United Kingdom which shows that to succeed at the upper levels, sponsorship is critical. Sponsored women are 52% more likely to be satisfied with their rate of advancement, 25% more likely to ask for a pay raise, and 58% less likely to plan on quitting within one year than those without a sponsor.

Hewlett believes that sponsorship can make up for women's incorrect impression that hard work will result in recognition. She states in an article in the *Harvard Business Review* blog[6] that "... hard work often does pay off for accomplished women—at least up until the middle rungs of management. But it's precisely at that point where who you know is just as important as how well you perform. The CTI research demonstrates that to break through to the top, well-qualified women everywhere need sponsors—powerful leaders who are willing to advocate for their next key role and propel and protect them through the perilous straits of upper management."

Women need to acquire these crucial relationships early in their careers and continue to cultivate them as they advance. But developing personal relationships with sponsors won't be enough to retain them. Women need to continue to benefit their sponsors by delivering loyalty and top performances. Even if a sponsor and protégé no longer work in the same area, an impressive protégé will reflect well on the sponsor who developed her.

Because a sponsor is a special type of mentor, you develop relationships similarly with both. You will want to be strategic about pursuing a strong sponsor relationship, though. Your sponsor will be the executive colleague most willing to open doors to senior officers and high-level assignments for you. She will be the mentor who you should focus most of your energy on.

NOTE TO FILE:

- **Gaining sponsorship requires a good bit of luck but won't happen unless you work hard on developing the relationship.**

Chapter 5: Performance Reviews: The Good, the Bad, and the Ugly

Whatever the problem, be part of the solution. Don't just sit around raising questions and pointing out obstacles.

—Tina Fey, *Bossypants*

Jay was a new associate at Merrill Lynch and older than most in that position. He had worked in another industry for several years before he switched over to banking. Senior officers in the group had given me feedback for Jay's upcoming performance review. He was a great team player when working on deals; he was reliably accurate and on time. And he was building the right skills to continue on the banking path. While the group agreed that Jay still didn't have the soft skills that were necessary to convey authority with clients, he was still ahead of most of his peers. They believed that if Jay were to model behavior of senior

officers and take some management training courses, he would have a great future in the industry.

When I conducted Jay's performance review, I conveyed the good impressions the senior officers had of him. Then I explained the steps that he would need to take to gain more influence and authority with clients.

"I disagree. I'm good with clients," Jay interrupted.

Yikes, I wasn't expecting that response. "You're very good with clients, Jay. They all like you and think you're doing a great job on their transactions. I'm referring to the next level of your development, involving the type of client interaction and influence you see the vice presidents or directors demonstrate."

"But I have that!" Jay shot back. "Look, you told me that clients like me. I'm old enough to be a vice president or director; I should be able to lead my own deals now! I'm not buying your crap about me needing to develop further."

Being anxious about your advancement is understandable, but Jay was looking at the whole review process in the wrong light. Reviews are designed to help employees perform better. At very senior levels they can turn into strategy sessions where colleagues discuss the best use of the reporting officer's talents to build business. The manager and the more junior professional should have the same goals: to develop the subordinate to advance his career and benefit the company.

Jay's review was a reflection of input from a variety of senior officers who had developed similar opinions of his strengths and weaknesses, yet Jay disagreed with their viewpoint. There are three problems with Jay's response. First, it's OK to believe that an evaluation of you is incorrect, but even if it is, you need to change others' perceptions. If you don't follow your manager's advice to make that change, you can come off as being defiant. So even if Jay thought the clients viewed him as an authoritative banker ready to run their deals, he could not convince senior bankers (who weren't ready to trust him to manage a transaction) unless he followed the development plan put in place for him.

Second, Jay refused great training that would be helpful for anyone hoping to advance at their company. In fact, many of the senior officers themselves probably had taken advantage of that training. And third, Jay should have tried to hide his anger and avoided using the "I'm not buying your crap" line. It wasn't a smart choice of words to direct at a reviewer, plus it made me have even less faith in his ability to handle clients independently. And, as you might have guessed...it ticked me off.

Even without anger, defensiveness doesn't play well in a review. In fact, an employee's defensiveness can signal to a manager that he is sensitive to negative feedback and the manager may stop giving it. Then the employee won't know where he is falling short and therefore can't try to work on correcting his weaknesses.

Although you may be sure you'll never come off as hot-headed as Jay, you may have a variety of frustrations that arise from performance reviews. Fortunately, you can minimize your distress and have a more productive meeting by planning ahead and knowing how to respond when you're given feedback.

Understand Expectations Early

Most disastrous review meetings are a result of misunderstood expectations and a lack of communication somewhere along the line. An employee can't fulfill her manager's expectations if she doesn't understand what he expects her to do. Problems will arise when a boss thinks he communicated his expectations clearly but he didn't, or when an employee assumes she understands his requests but she doesn't. In those cases, when the manager discusses his subordinate's under-performance in her review, she will be hurt, angry, and skeptical about his evaluation. The employee will wonder why her boss waited a year to bring up these issues if he believes they are as significant as he says they are. Plus, now his assessment is on her permanent record and she didn't even know that she was making mistakes. Had she understood her manager's expectations early on, she would have been better able to fulfill them.

My friend Shana took over as general manager of a distribution facility with about 300 employees. Soon after she arrived she noticed that if the receptionist was busy trying to grab a file or finish up an e-mail, she would let the phone ring up to five times before she answered it. Shana told the receptionist that customers call frequently and she had to be very responsive. In particular, she needed to answer within two rings. The receptionist thought for a second and replied, "Thanks. No one ever told me that. It makes complete sense."

Unfortunately, many managers expect their employees, like Shana's receptionist, to be clairvoyant. Nonetheless, it's every individual's own responsibility to understand their supervisor's expectations. Even if you think you know, ask. Find out your manager's objectives and which of those are most important to her. Discuss specific elements of these goals, such as how you will be measured and what your targets will be. If you have some quantifiable tasks, such as *increase in click-throughs on your digital marketing campaign*, find out what the target number is for outstanding performance. If your manager simply tells you to make some *headway* on your digital marketing campaign, try to pin her down and have her define what she means by "headway."

One of your company's and your boss's primary objectives may be more qualitative, such as *teamwork*. Don't assume you know what that means. Maybe you need to go out of your way to brainstorm with colleagues during the project instead of completing your portion of the assignment on your own. Ask your boss for examples of excellent teamwork from her viewpoint, and ask whether you need to meet as a team when it would be faster to work alone.

Make sure you understand the difference between expected behavior and outstanding work. For instance, producing flawless work and meeting deadlines may be tough duty, but your manager might consider it expected behavior for which she'll award you mediocre ratings. Maybe superior ratings would require beating deadlines or innovation on your part. If you're going to work your tail off, you might as well figure out if your efforts will improve your standing at the office.

And since your performance review is part of your permanent record, you can't be too diligent about making sure your manager's priorities haven't changed throughout the year. Check in every once in a while to ensure that selling 1,600 widgets a month is still her goal for you. From her perspective, it could be that widgets went out and doodads came in, and she forgot to tell you.

NOTE TO FILE: 

- Make sure you understand your individual project leader's expectations, too. Your manager will ask for her input at review time.
- Expected behavior doesn't necessarily equal outstanding performance.

Reviews: Groundhog Day Style

Studies[1] document that pretty much everyone hates performance reviews. Even though development is the goal, people just don't like to be criticized. And pre-review jitters can be worse than the actual event. Employees anticipate criticism but also worry that their manager is biased or wrong about their performance. So wouldn't you think reducing the number of your reviews would help you live a longer, less stressed life? Surprisingly, you will achieve way more zen-ness if you ask for feedback as often as possible.

Sounds counterintuitive, right? You might understand better if you think of it like any kind of coaching you've ever received, either for sports, a musical instrument, a theatrical performance, or even academics. You didn't get upset when your basketball coach told you to follow through when you shoot. She may have even reminded you at every practice you had. You tried but didn't always remember to apply your coach's advice, so you didn't mind when she repeated herself. Now can you imagine if you played ball all year round with your coach watching you but not giving you any tips until the end of the year? At that point, the two of you would get together and she would list everything you had done wrong for the past 12 months. "Oh remember that game against Springfield eight months ago?" she would say. "What were you thinking in the first quarter when you threw to Lani? Sarah was wide open!" If you had a meeting and a relationship like that with your coach you would probably dread your meeting as much as you might dread an annual performance review.

Even if your company has a policy of one review a year for each employee, you can dilute the potentially massive impact of that one meeting by asking for coaching throughout the year. Tell your boss you would like her to give you tips on anything you could do to perform your job better, whenever she notices room for improvement. But don't rely on her always following through; during or after a project, ask her for suggestions. Other managers, not just your boss, may have ideas for you as well so let them know you are open to hearing their thoughts.

When you seek frequent feedback from others, two things happen to make your review a more pleasant experience. First, you receive continuous suggestions that you act on, reducing the amount of negative feedback at your review. Second, you become much more accustomed to receiving constructive criticism and won't be insulted, hurt, or angered at suggestions that previously may have upset you.

As you rise in your organization and are managing your own groups of employees, the same principles will apply, but you might interact with your boss a little differently. You could ask him how he thought your client pitch went and if he had any suggestions for your next pitch. It all sounds more strategic, but you're basically asking for performance feedback just as you did earlier in your career.

One of my former colleagues once told me that he was worried about his wife. "Asha rarely speaks to her manager," he said. "It's tough because he spends two weeks a month in the London office, but I don't understand why she hasn't gotten together with him when he's back at the home office. Asha's so stressed lately; I think it's because she doesn't know where she stands at work. At least she promised me she would get on her boss's schedule during his next trip back here."

A month later my colleague came into my office and told me his wife had been fired. "Remember I told you that Asha was going to talk to her boss?" he asked. "Her boss's assistant told Asha that his schedule was crammed. Asha didn't want to push. I told her she should camp outside his office until they found time for her. I mean, there has to be 15 minutes in the two weeks he's there that he can see her. Instead Asha decided she'd wait until the next trip. The next time her boss returned, he called her into his office and terminated her. She doesn't even understand why. Her boss said they were restructuring but three of her peers were saved. He's an awful communicator, but she knows it was partly her fault."

Asha didn't make the same mistake at her next company. She met with her boss and casually asked for feedback every time she met with him. As a result, she moved up quickly at her new job.

Checking in frequently would be easier if companies embraced that approach and encouraged managers to adopt it. Adobe Systems did just that. It institutionalized a more casual approach to feedback.[2] The company abolished yearly performance reviews in favor of frequent "check-ins" where managers coach employees on an unspecified schedule. The goal is to give employees the advice they need when it's relevant so that they can act on it to improve performance.

Although the traditional annual review has been much maligned by business theorists, Adobe has been one of the few companies to do away with the standard. So if you don't happen to be working at Adobe, the best way to simulate the benefits of its practice is to ask for feedback yourself.

Self-Evaluations

Some companies require their employees to fill out self-evaluations annually. Although these reports are tedious to complete, a lot could be riding on them. Managers might use them to prepare performance reports, determine pay increases, or make promotion decisions. But even if your organization doesn't make you complete an assessment every year, you should keep a record of your achievements so you can talk about them with your manager at your review or on other occasions.

If you wait until review time comes around, you're likely to have forgotten some of your accomplishments, so take notes during the year. Create a file that lists projects and relevant figures, such as sales numbers or increased market penetration percentages. The more hard data you can compile, the better. Record what you accomplished on your assignments, highlighting when you over-performed and solutions you created. Make sure to mention efforts you made to address any development issues raised by your manager in the past. And don't forget to add extra work-related commitments like *campus interviewer for division* or *member of Technology Steering Committee*. Just keep the file handy all year, whether it's a physical file or a file on your computer, add to it whenever you complete a project or even when someone gives you a compliment that you realize meant you accomplished something unique. My office mate once told me she was glad she kept a file. She had forgotten a quick revenue-related assignment she had completed ten months before until she looked over her recorded list. When she mentioned it in her review her boss said, "Oh that was you? I thought it was Jada. Thanks for clearing that up."

The file will be a good reference for filling out your evaluation. You can review it when the form asks you to assess how you performed in certain areas. Being honest about your achievements is important, so take ownership if you believe that you performed exceptionally. A large portion of the self-evaluation should be positive, but a totally maxed-out assessment may not be taken as seriously as one that mentions one or two areas for development. Everyone can improve and acknowledgment of your need to improve will show you are self-aware. When you refer to an area that you need to develop, make sure you include your game plan showing how you intend to achieve it.

Also try to weave your career goals into your write-up to make sure your manager understands them and to kick-start a conversation. Discuss where you would like to be in the next few years and ask your manager her thoughts on how you can get there. Ask her for her help in project selection and let her know you would like to hear about any opportunities that can help you achieve your goals. Are you open to a move to another city or country? Let your manager know or she may assume otherwise.

NOTE TO FILE: 

- Managers also use self-evaluations to see if they made their objectives clear.
- Managers believe forcing employees to review their work helps them to acknowledge and develop.

Prepare Emotionally and Strategically

If you have asked for frequent feedback, chances are you won't need to prepare for a stress-inducing review, especially if you've acted on suggestions you've been given. But since it's handy to be ready for all circumstances, it's best to plan for the worst. Reviews can incite all sorts of emotions including fear, anger, sadness, hurt, and distrust. If you can envision review-day scenarios, you will be better equipped to eliminate an emotionally charged discussion with your boss.

Some companies use review metrics including **rank order assessments** or **numerical rankings.** Rank order assessments, also called **stack rankings,** compare you with your peers and let you know how you match up. Managers who complete rank order assessments must place employees in categories limited by percentages. For instance, they might need to distribute their reports on a scale so that no more than 15 percent could appear in the "top" category and no more than 15 percent could appear in the "good" category, and so on. So if your company employs a ranking system, consider how you will respond at your review if the category you are in is lower than you hoped. Visualizing disappointment ahead of time will help you be better prepared should it occur. At the meeting, ask your manager how he interprets the number and focus on his development plan—not your rank.

A numerical ranking won't compare you to your peers but it will rank your performance and different skills on a scale. A "3" on a 5-point scale could be the maximum your manager ever awards, so prepare yourself to see low-looking numbers. Again, ask your boss what your numbers mean and how you can raise them. Even if he "never gives a 5," he ought to be able to tell you the feats you'd have to accomplish to earn one. Who knows, maybe you can surprise him.

Overall, it's best to realize that everyone can improve in some way and you will likely be told you need to also. If it makes you feel better, your manager's boss is telling her the same thing. Before the meeting, acknowledging that your manager will make development suggestions should make you more ready to hear them. Anticipate what your boss will highlight as problem areas and be ready with possible solutions. Will she tell you you're too quiet in meetings? If so, tell her you plan to speak up more and ask if you can attend meetings more frequently to increase your comfort level.

NOTE TO FILE: 

- Visualize the worst-case scenario and how you would respond to prepare for your review.
- Your boss's **perceptions are reality** when it concerns your review.

The Review

During the review, remember your manager is a coach of sorts. She will instruct you on the best way to succeed; you should incorporate her tips into the way you play the game. You're both on the same team with shared goals: to foster your development and to help your unit and company succeed. But each of you prioritizes the goals differently. Your boss will be more concerned with success in the organization because it reflects on her record, and you will be focused foremost on your performance. So keep in mind your boss's perspective during your review. Talk about your development, but tie it in to the goals of her department and the company.

Listen

Your first role during your review is to listen, but not for obvious reasons. Yes, you need to listen to your boss's evaluation but more importantly, you need to listen to what he doesn't say. Many managers can't stomach delivering bad news. They may give only good news or soft-pedal bad news by mentioning it quickly. So listen carefully to any suggestions. If your boss doesn't highlight any areas for improvement, ask the question yourself. You could even prompt him by asking him to critique specific skills that you're concerned about. The worst outcome of a review would be for you to lose out on a promotion, pay raise, or important project because you weren't aware of issues that were holding you back.

If he tells you something negative about your performance, don't disagree. Listen and discuss it professionally. But if discussing the topic upsets you to the point of causing you to become emotional, just listen to your boss and come back to the subject at a later meeting. Then you can calmly ask questions and talk about an improvement plan.

Clarify

When you're given advice to improve your performance, you need to understand the issues that caused the problem and the best way to do that is to ask questions. In one of my reviews, my manager told me that a Latin American client had complained that my style was too aggressive. I reminded my boss that my client, in his 50s, had a wife in her 20s, and I noted that perhaps he preferred working with women he could dominate. In retrospect, I guess I didn't give the most helpful reply. My manager didn't know how to respond and moved on. Yes, he should have discussed the issue further, but since he didn't, I should have asked him what specific instances caused the problem. It was my manager's job to investigate any concern raised. I focused on blaming my client because I suspected that my behavior would not have been considered aggressive had a man been in the same situation. But by neglecting to get details, I wasn't able to determine how I could have interacted with my client more effectively.

When you do ask questions or seek your manager's advice, focus on the specific things that you should improve. If you manage quality control and your manager wants you to reduce product defects, ask him what percentage he wants you to decrease them by. Would that target be meeting or exceeding expectations? Continue to ask questions until you understand your manager's specific objectives.

Gender-Influenced Development Issues

The previous story about my client may make you wonder about raising the issue of gender bias at work. Should I have discussed the gender-based inequity with regard to the way the client viewed me? If I did, would I help my boss understand that I didn't act any differently than any other on his team might have? Would that knowledge have allowed him to have a better opinion of me? These are tricky questions because some managers may acknowledge gender bias, while others won't be able to see it. One thing is certain: if you are in a situation like I was in, your boss will be most concerned about you fixing the relationship problem. If you have shown that you will work toward that objective with no signs of frustration, you may improve his understanding of the situation by raising the question of inequity.

Posing a question about the situation would be the best approach because it eliminates the possibility that you will come off sounding defensive or bitter. Ask your boss if he thinks there is a possibility that your client might not have raised the same concerns if you had been a man. If he is responsive to the thought, you have made him understand the situation a bit better and that understanding may raise his opinion of you. But if he disagrees, you won't gain by arguing. Your goal should be to improve your reputation in his eyes, not impair it.

There is a potential downside to raising the topic as well. You may highlight a cultural issue that could cause your boss to change coverage for the client. He might determine that the client will have problems with any woman and decide to assign a man to the account. Or your manager may think about other clients who could feel similarly and think twice about assigning you to them. I would like to think that managers would not make those kinds of decisions, but in reality, some will. So there are no easy answers as to how you approach the situation. You will have to decide based upon what you think will be the most likely impact of that conversation with your manager.

Your Development Plan

During your review, you've learned the areas you need to work on, including your boss's specific objectives for you. Next you have to discuss how to attack the problems with your manager. Some goals may be straightforward, like *work more on meeting deadlines,* but others will merit more thought. If your manager wants you to gain more exposure through public speaking, enlist his help. Do you need training or do you just need more opportunities? Can he recommend industry conferences to attend and help you land some panelist slots?

After you have a development plan set, repeat it to your boss to allow him one more chance to offer input.

Goals and Accomplishments

Your review shouldn't be all critique without a discussion of your accomplishments and career goals. Some companies tie salary and promotion discussions into reviews, and others purposefully don't. At my firm, managers separated reviews from bonus discussions because, bankers being bankers, they would want to talk about nothing but pay during their performance review.

Regardless of whether your review covers pay and promotion, it never hurts to discuss accomplishments and goals with your boss. If you handed in a self-evaluation, your boss has a list of your accomplishments. You may want to ask her if she has any questions or comments about them. As we discussed earlier, your manager, whether a mentor or not, can give you valuable support in pursuing your career. Ask her for her thoughts and discuss your ideas with her.

Request and Reconvene

Before you leave your manager's office, make sure you understand your development plan going forward. Also, you might want to ask for immediate feedback when your manager notices a need for improvement. Tell her that you'd like to know right away if she has any suggestions regarding how you could do something better. Make sure she understands you can take her constructive criticism; your goals require you to perform at a high level and you need her help to reach them.

Lastly, tell your boss you'd like to catch up with her in a month to go over your progress. She'll be happy to agree. All you have to do is schedule the meeting.

Chapter 6: From Expert to Powerhouse

Don't follow the crowd, let the crowd follow you.

—Margaret Thatcher

Kathleen McCartney began her new job as President of Smith College with a Listening Tour across the nation. She wanted to hear from the school's alumnae on important issues facing women's colleges and Smith specifically. "A leader would be ill-advised to develop a strategic plan on the day she takes office," Kathy told me a few hours before her meeting with Washington, D.C.–based Smith graduates.

Kathy learned in her prior role as Dean of the Harvard Graduate School of Education that leadership ". . . is all about ***retail politics.*** *If you are a leader, you need to explore the hopes, dreams, and concerns of all stakeholders." Using that strategy, she and her team created an innovative doctoral degree program at Harvard involving three professional schools: the Graduate School of Education, the Business School, and the Kennedy*

School. This was the first program that offered a doctorate of education leadership to provide training for educators in leadership and management, politics and policymaking, and, of course, education. She brainstormed with her senior leadership team as well as faculty colleagues to develop the concept. "You always want to be as bottom up as possible," Kathy reflected, "so that the voices of all stakeholders are heard from the beginning; this builds support going forward. Top down management, where leaders make decisions in a vacuum, doesn't work."

What Is a Powerhouse?

In her role as dean and president, Kathy McCartney has demonstrated some important leadership skills, especially **listening to and engaging team members.** Additional management skills that she and other leaders possess include **competency and innovation, comfort in the face of ambiguity, sending clear messages,** and **influencing up and down the organization.**

Listening and Engaging Team Members

I attended a leadership course at Merrill Lynch where bankers read an account about a small aircraft crash landing in wilderness territory, 150 miles from civilization. The only passenger was the pilot, who survived. The story described the items in the pilot's pockets and showed us a map of the area. It also gave us day and nighttime temperature ranges and described the animals and vegetation in the area.

Our leadership instructor told us to break into groups and come up with a survival plan for the lost pilot. We learned there was a correct answer, meaning we had to make proper use of pocket contents, edible plants, and common sense or our pilot would die of sun stroke, starvation, or snake bite. We were also competing with the other leadership teams to see who could come up with, if not the correct answer, the one closest to it.

I figured losing a game in leadership training would be a bad omen for my career, so I was thrilled to discover that one of my teammates would be an ex-Navy SEAL. We couldn't lose with a Special Forces operative on our team! The ex-SEAL took charge immediately and told us how the pilot was going to reach civilization. The rest of us proposed suggestions to tweak the strategy but our ex-SEAL teammate explained why most of our ideas wouldn't work. We deferred to the teammate who had experienced so much more than any of us, and gladly adopted our military-inspired survival plan.

As it turned out, we didn't win or even come in second. We ranked third out of the five leadership teams. In fact, we inadvertently killed off our pilot and lost the competition despite having the only team member trained in extreme survival tactics. Our leadership instructor wasn't surprised. He told us that no matter how skilled one member of a team is, it's proven that the most collaborative teams are those that generally win. And one strong leader who doesn't listen or respond to team members' suggestions will typically worsen the outcome.

For the same reason, thoughtful leaders build teams with members who have complementary abilities. Ideally a great team has a mix of visionaries and detail-oriented thinkers.

Effective leaders also often rely on the workers closest to the product or service for input. The men and women on the assembly line may make better conclusions than the plant manager about why manufacturing times increased. Similarly, leaders know that salespeople often have the best information on whether a product needs changes. If a manager doesn't dig deep into her organization to tap the knowledge and experiences of the workers, she can't make the best decisions for her group.

A great by-product of a leader who listens and engages with employees at all levels is motivation. Team members are much more willing to work toward a common goal if they believe they have contributed to the strategy adopted. An effective manager who doesn't see much value in a subordinate's suggestions might even allow her to pursue her plan to build camaraderie. As a result, the next time the manager wants buy-in on her own plan, the subordinate will be more enthusiastic.

And part of engaging is delegating any job that a manager can pass on. Robert Sapolsky, Stanford neuroscientist, in his book *Why Zebras Don't Get Ulcers,*[1] states that "Most studies have shown that it is middle management that succumbs to the stress-related diseases. This is thought to reflect the killer combination that these folks are often burdened with, namely, high work demands but little autonomy—responsibility without control." Even if they don't analyze the stress/control relationship, great leaders know to empower their team members. Giving authority to others increases their job satisfaction and self-worth, creating better outcomes for everyone.

Competency and Innovation

A leader needs to be competent in his field to influence his team and move them forward into action. He demonstrates raw intellect and command of the skills necessary to lead. If his employees question his knowledge, they may ignore his plan. They may also become frustrated that someone less competent than themselves is directing them.

A skill base is necessary for all leaders, but exceptional ones are innovative and visionary. They can see possibilities and create solutions that others may not be able to develop. These are the type of managers who create new products or strategies and leave most of us wondering how they came up with those unique ideas. They inspire their teams, making members want to be involved in their leader's projects.

Comfort in the Face of Ambiguity

Being able to make decisions without full information is an essential skill in today's changing business environment. To make those decisions requires both knowledge, to help you piece together useful information, and an aptitude for risk. With technology and globalization becoming increasingly important factors in business, situations will arise without precedents and without answers. Successful leaders draw on their experiences and feel comfortable directing strategy when future outcomes are unclear. They have an outsized ability to cope, are able to maintain their composure under pressure, and are decisive enough to take action.

Elyse Allan, CEO of General Electric Canada, a unit of the fourth-largest public company in the world,[2] told me that "Clear thinking allows leaders to connect the dots to develop a plan when challenges arise. Courage lets them put that plan in place." Elyse said her company particularly values those qualities. When an executive from G.E. interviewed her for her current job, he conveyed that the position was evolving and had a different scope of responsibilities than it had in the past. He highlighted that G.E. wanted a new type of leader to take over. Elyse understood what he was looking for. She wrote him a post-interview note saying "I am totally comfortable with the complete ambiguity of the job you tried to describe." He must have agreed.

Clear Message and Ability to Influence

You may have noticed at your company that good leaders deliver clear messages. It's hard to gain support if your team doesn't understand you. The best managers also create emotional connections with their colleagues. They inspire team members by setting solid examples and by conveying the benefits of the mission. But they have to influence company executives as well. Effective leaders develop 360° dialogues to move projects forward.

Lieutenant General Patrick Donahue, Deputy Commanding General at U.S. Army Forces Command, has led tens of thousands of troops in his career in peace and war. He conveyed to me that "leaders have an ability to get things done. Those who have influence up and down an organization will be able to impose their will. But they also need to have drive; they need to tirelessly push their ideas until their organization accepts and embraces them."

NOTE TO FILE: 

- About $12 billion[3] is spent annually by U.S. companies on leadership development.
- The number of women board members has grown faster[4] and exceeded, on a percentage basis, the number of women in executive positions at Fortune 500 companies.

How You Become a Powerhouse

When you are in the Expert stage of your career, you will rise to become a Powerhouse if you demonstrate that you can operate at the next level. But what exactly does acting like a Powerhouse mean? Although the stereotypical image of a leader is a professional with a big voice and even bigger personality, leaders are both extroverts and introverts. Or at least they have tendencies toward one personality type or the other. As noted psychotherapist Carl Jung reflected, "There is no such thing as a pure introvert or extrovert. Such a person would be in the lunatic asylum."[5] A recent Harvard Business School/North Carolina Keenan Flagler Business School study[6] revealed that leaders of each personality type can be effective; their influence depends on the type of people they are managing. Extroverted leaders are able to work better with more passive employees because the pair would be less prone to personality clashes. Introverted managers tend to be more effective with proactive employees who benefit from their manager's skill in listening and analyzing team ideas.

Many successful people appear to have been **born to lead,** but others have had to develop the necessary skills to manage teams and influence colleagues. One thing is certain: those who want to become leaders will increase their chances to do so by working to improve those skills.

Executive Presence

My job required me to travel with my clients to raise institutional equity funds. Unlike asking for capital for a company with real products or services, we were raising money for blind pool funds. These funds were "trust-me" financial vehicles. The investors would meet my client who had a track record of successful company investments. If the investors warmed to my client and liked his story, they would meet with him and his team many more times and then initiate due diligence procedures to vet my client's past performance. This process could take anywhere from a few months to a year. The best outcome for my client would be an investment, sometimes upward of $100 million from one investor.

As you can imagine, to persuade investors from state pension funds or corporations that they should invest in a blind pool, my clients had to be convincing. They also had to be charismatic, poised, brilliant, and charming. One particular client, Sam Zell, is all that and more. Sam is a real-estate and corporate investor, known in finance circles as "The Grave Dancer" because he seeks dying companies, buys them, turns them around, and sells them for an impressive profit. At the time I was raising funds for Sam's investment vehicle, he owned and operated more commercial real estate in the United States than any other entity, except the U.S. government.

Sam may have had a reputation as a 5-foot-5-inch, bald-headed, foul-mouthed corporate raider, but our investors loved him. He walked into a meeting and his eyes lit up when he greeted the hosts. If he had ever met an investor before, he remembered her as well as their conversation. I would hand Sam a stack of Merrill

Lynch–prepared presentation books, and he would throw them to the side and start his presentation without glancing at them again. Sam looked the investors right in the eye and carefully answered any questions they had. He told them their questions showed they had terrific insight; coming from a man commonly referred to as a visionary, the investors felt especially smart after receiving his compliment. One of Sam's favorite pastimes was making jokes at his investment banker's expense, which ingratiated him to the investors even more. Of course everyone likes bashing bankers. He told investors in Tokyo that in preparation for the trip to Japan I had supplied him with business cards written in Chinese. He knew how to work the crowd.

Sam epitomized executive presence during our investor meetings. His business success, reflected by his ranking as number 110 on Forbes 400 list,[7] relies on Sam's vision, his appetite for risk, and his intellect. But without the ability to win over investors, sellers, buyers, and his employees, his success would not have been possible.

Executive presence is the bearing of a poised, confident leader—credible and inspirational to her team, reliable and trustworthy to her organization. Many characteristics of executive presence are similar to the soft skills that you began to develop at the start of your career. And since many of these personal skills will improve with time, starting early will help you throughout your career. But unlike earlier advances, jumping from the Expert to the Powerhouse stage will rely most heavily on your display of executive presence. The standards will be higher too. You may set yourself apart as a New Careerist by your ability to perform well under deadlines, but 15 years later as a leader in your organization, you—and any other leader—will need to broaden your coping skills as you make decisions and form strategy during difficult and challenging situations. Executive presence needed to gain leadership positions requires a deeper command of the underlying skills and includes a greater breath of personal skills than you have had to master before in your career.

Controlling and Reading Emotions. You may have demonstrated self-confidence and poise as a New Careerist, but as a leader you have to develop those traits even more. A leader needs to maintain composure when under fire from colleagues and clients. She needs to be able to defend her actions or accept blame for herself and her team with grace and maturity, even when others are emotional. Keeping a cool head will gain a leader respect from her associates.

Along with controlling her own emotions, an effective leader is able to read subtle emotions of others and respond appropriately. This area of leadership is one in which women should be particularly skilled at developing. Studies[8] have shown that women have larger gray matter volumes in brain regions related to processing social cues than do men. So a woman's gender serves her well in interpreting an employee's response. The executive may need to detect resistance to a plan to determine how to best motivate her team. Alternatively, she may need to determine why an employee seems to have become less productive. The manager's ability to empathize and connect with her employee base is necessary for her to inspire her team members and incent them to follow her leadership.

Be Authentic. Those with executive presence also project credibility, integrity, and authenticity. During their careers, leaders gain knowledge and a track record of successes, which make them credible figures of authority in their fields. If they also exhibit integrity and authenticity in all they do, employees will look to them for direction and guidance. Being an authentic leader may seem like the natural path to take, but women sometimes have difficulty pulling it off. We often don't have many female role models so we try to determine the best mix of our own personal style and that of our male leaders. When Janet Piller, Chief Administrative Officer of an international development institution, began to manage a large number of employees, she thought she needed to appear more solemn and less approachable to be taken seriously. But her adopted style didn't fit her personality. She's friendly by nature, and when she tried to appear more authoritative, she couldn't connect with her employees. Janet found managing her team much easier after she returned to her authentic style.

Communication Style. Communication style is another differentiator between leaders and those who can't make that jump. Leaders are succinct and concise and speak with authority. They are comfortable thinking on their feet and debating complex issues. They don't have to be loud or overbearing but their tone should be appropriately assertive. Women especially can struggle with how assertive they should sound; today's business world has a narrower acceptable range for women than men in that regard. Often, women either appear too aggressive and bossy or too passive and self-deprecating. Again, authenticity is critical, but many women leaders find that pushing the boundaries of comfortable behavior will help them appear in control. Some talk louder than they might otherwise so they aren't ignored. They interrupt in an effective manner to develop a point. They hold their own with colleagues who forcefully argue against them, all the while looking comfortable, not intimidated.

Another important aspect of communication for leaders is body language, and posture tops the list. You recognize reticence and insecurity immediately when you see a slouching person at the office or a slumped-over stranger on the street. You get a sense that these people lack confidence, even without hearing them utter a word. Your body language needs to be positive, just like your attitude. Stand tall and make eye contact without looking down. Deliver a firm handshake and smile. Carry yourself in an open position, without crossing your arms, to convey openness to others. None of this may be new information to you, but you may need to be more aware of what your body language is saying. Many people don't realize the message they are sending. Ask a trusted friend how she thinks you carry yourself to find out if you need to work on your image.

Your Appearance Counts. Your appearance is a final, but important element of executive presence. Leaders need to dress like leaders, which means tastefully fashionable, yet conservative. If you know you've got the conservative part of it down, make sure your clothes are tailored well; not too loose or they could come off as frumpy or outdated. Clothing that is way out of style will make it hard for you to command respect as a leader. I saw a woman on a train recently who dressed in a style I would describe as "retro-librarian." Her skirt hung mid-calf and was made of a heavy green tweed material. She also wore a matching wool sweater jacket. Then I saw she held a briefcase and had a fashionably dressed co-worker traveling with her. The librarian look-alike was much older than her colleague, yet the younger woman was clearly the senior professional. The older woman didn't convey the impression of an executive because of her overly-conservative non-businesslike style choices. I would guess the look she adopted also slowed her advancement at her company.

If overly conservative is not your problem, ask yourself if your clothes might be too tight or provocative. If you look at top women leaders worldwide, you'll notice that their clothing has one thing in common: it's not distracting. Exceptional workers who don't dress appropriately often don't realize they have an image problem. Asking a put-together peer about your look should help you gauge whether you need to make changes.

How Others Perceive You. Since executive presence is so critical to making the jump to the Powerhouse stage, make sure you're on top of how others perceive you. You can ask senior managers on your project or peers whom you trust. Ask your office mate how she thought your presentation went, and you might discover that you don't make eye contact when you're addressing groups.

Self-awareness is the first step toward improving your performance. Aileen Richards, Executive Vice President and Head of Human Resources at Mars Incorporated, believes that at the upper tiers, the ability to acknowledge room for improvement of your personal skills will lead to advancement. "Nearly everyone has functional competence," she states. "What characterizes successful professionals are the soft skills: people skills, self-awareness, the desire to change as an individual and respond to feedback."

But can you learn soft skills? Absolutely! You can always pursue training, but one of the most effective ways to learn how to act like an executive is to observe one you work with. Notice the way colleagues respond to questions, give directions, or disagree with others. You'll be able to model the behavior that feels right for you, which will help you develop into a leader.

Highlighting Your Assets

Executives at a pension fund advisory company where my friend Allison works often pull her into difficult client situations. Allison has developed the reputation of being able to reduce tensions in a room full of hot tempers. This skill has made her indispensable to her organization and has helped her advance to become one of its senior consultants.

Everyone should highlight their unique combination of soft and functional (or job-related) skills, if they want to advance from the Expert to the Powerhouse stage. As you progress in your career, try to develop your best personality assets, but also focus on acquiring functional skills that will differentiate you. These skills could range from having an unusual ability to forecast new product sales growth or being able to turn around a failing business. But to master any job-related ability, you will need to gain the experiences needed to acquire them. So as you develop your plan to climb to the next level, consider how you can bring **signature** knowledge and skills to your job.

And make sure you seek occasions to demonstrate the skills you have developed. One of the most valuable contributions a professional can make is to offer a solution to a problem. Either bring attention to the issue yourself or resolve one that a manager identifies. You will become a problem solver in your company, which is a great reputation to have for someone targeting a leadership position.

NOTE TO FILE:

- Develop distinctive skills. Offer solutions.
- Don't be afraid to tackle problems. Failure serves as the best teacher.

Women-Specific Challenges and Success Criteria

My manager introduced me once to another colleague saying, "I don't know how she does it. She has two children in diapers, runs every morning, and is managing more deals than anyone in the group."

Guilty as charged. I wouldn't have changed a thing about that description except the last part. I had accepted too many assignments and it was hard to effectively manage all of them. But that's what women do. They have difficulty saying no. In a study[9] reported in the *WSJ*, female undergraduates were 50% more likely to comply with a request for a favor than their male peers.

Especially in the Expert stage, when a woman's goal is to become a leader, she tends to agree to do everything thrown at her. Sometimes part of the work is helping out a colleague and sometimes it's doing what her boss asked her to do. But women should be aware that taking on a huge workload is a tradeoff that may not be worthwhile. Their work may suffer or they might not have the opportunity to work on building strong client and colleague relationships. And certainly they'll feel less in control, which will make them unhappy and less productive at work.

Women also hear that when they self-promote they sound egocentric. That's a significant problem because some form of self-promotion, as men have discovered, is crucial. When you let your manager know what you've done, put it in the context of describing a project or a successful outcome. You will have described your role and your accomplishments without putting off your manager. Also, use your networks to help you out. If you compliment your colleagues on their work in front of their managers, they will be likely to do the same for you. Your clients or superiors in other parts of the company might put a good word in for you, too.

Interestingly, despite the challenges women leaders face, two leading studies indicate that top women professionals surpass men in the vast majority of leadership traits. The Zenger/Folkman study[10] identifies 16 traits of leadership and how women and men leaders are perceived. Women topped men in all categories except "develops strategic perspective." The authors of the study explain that women's lower marks on that measure result, in part, from fewer women in CEO ranks, the position where professionals exhibit the most strategic vision.

Similarly, a Caliper Corporation study[11] showed that women leaders scored significantly higher on persuasiveness, assertiveness, willingness to assume risk, empathy, urgency, flexibility, and sociability. Men leaders scored higher on thoroughness, cautiousness, and adhering to procedures. Lower relative marks on cautiousness, thoroughness, and adhering to procedures actually may have reflected the women's need to take the risks that were necessary to outshine their male competitors.

Reflecting on the research results, Dr. Thomas Schoenfelder, Senior Vice President of Research and Development at Caliper, told me that "Our most recent studies show that personality traits, behavior, and self-motivation can tell us a lot. These factors determine a woman's potential to be a highly effective leader. They also illuminate how successful women overcome obstacles to get promoted. For example, we found that women who are able to conquer gender stereotypes, which often reduce one's motivation to lead, employ a straightforward communication style, persevere in the face of challenges, take calculated risks, avoid being overly accommodating to others, and are comfortable bypassing rules to accomplish goals."

It has been difficult for women to reach leadership positions as it is, and the ones who have prevailed have had to display stellar management abilities. Tom explained that "Caliper's studies reveal that successful women leaders tend to motivate by getting team members to take ownership of company and department goals, strategies, and values. That is, they tend to be better at getting participation, engagement, and true buy-in for the mission at hand. The women leaders we studied were more interested in hearing all points of view, before making the best possible decision. The final decision did not necessarily have to be their initial point of view. They were able to read situations accurately and take in information from all sides, then make the most informed decision possible." The research indicated that male leaders, on the other hand, tended to force their point of view and be less flexible, pushing their ideas home, potentially causing backlash in the future.

The study results underscore that certain personality traits and behavior will help you rise to top management positions. Fortunately, you can develop many of those qualities on your own or with training during your career. But the research also tells us that highly successful women possess leadership skills prevalent in their gender. Businesses today need leaders with a woman's distinctive assets. Be a leader, but be one in a way that feels authentic and allows you to have maximum impact with your team and organization.

NOTE TO FILE: 

- Reasons women don't say "No" to too much work: they put others' needs first, they want to be liked, they don't want to be rude, they're afraid of conflict, they fear a superior's displeasure, and they want to demonstrate that they're team players.

Foster the People

One of the most important jobs of a Powerhouse, of course, is to lead. Your team will rely on you for direction and guidance regarding their work and their careers. To help as their leader, you need to delegate to your capable employees as well as develop those who are not ready for more responsibility. Delegating can be difficult; your employees will make mistakes. But as they do, they will learn. Even if they start to go down the wrong path, resist the temptation to take over their tasks. Allowing your subordinates to manage their work independently will leverage your time, create a more effective team, and make each of you more valuable.

One of my direct reports, Michelle, once updated me on a project she was managing. She complained that her analyst, Brian, hadn't finished the numbers and she had to take over his work.

"You gave him a deadline and he didn't meet it?" I asked.

"Not exactly," Michelle replied. "I checked on him this morning and he hadn't started. I needed the numbers by 2 p.m., so I told him I would do them."

"So, he could have gotten them done?"

"I think so, but he was working on another project and I wasn't sure if he would run into trouble. I need them for the client meeting at 4 p.m.," Michelle responded.

"Is Brian going to the client meeting, too?" I asked.

"Well I was going to ask him, but now that he hasn't done the numbers, he won't add much value, will he?"

I guess Brian wouldn't add value because Michelle didn't give him the opportunity to. Brian was a capable modeler and could easily have spread the numbers in time. Michelle's tendency to micromanage tied up her time in a role that was not a good use of her talents and eliminated an opportunity for Brian to learn about interacting with clients. By taking away his responsibility and complaining about Brian to me, Michelle fell short as a manager. A good leader finds ways to praise her subordinates and motivate them, not throw them under the bus.

Leaders also capitalize on their employees' talents. Highlighting your subordinate's strengths helps him gain visibility within your company and helps you leverage your own time. Of course you need to keep an eye on bolstering other areas a subordinate might have that are weak, but let him build confidence by displaying his best skills. You might feel better delegating if you staff two subordinates with complementary skills together; that way they can learn from each other.

Lastly, leaders encourage teamwork and they support and fight for their people. Those you manage will be the happiest and most productive if they work together as a team. Motivate them to work for a common goal and correct those who put their own interests first. The more effective they are as team members, the less time you will need to manage and the more time you will be able to put toward strategy, problem solving, and production. So as you develop your people, realize they will make mistakes and will learn from them. You are allowing them to be better performers. They may also come under fire from others and you need to support them, even to your superiors. Whether it is pay, promotion, or lay-off decisions, they are your people and if you believe in them, you should fight for them. They will know that you did.

Chapter 7: *Want It? Ask for It!*

Power's not given to you. You have to take it.

—Beyoncé

Vicky Neilson, a brand management executive in the cosmetics industry, had been working on the Bath & Body Works business for four years as a marketing director at Gryphon Development, a venture that created personal-care businesses for Limited Brands. Vicky had heard that Disney had approached Gryphon about developing an exclusive personal-care business for The Disney Store and decided she wanted to be a part of the new project. She talked to her boss about her idea but he was skeptical that she could handle it. "You know this would be creating the brand from scratch, right?" he asked. When she told him she understood, he said she could create the pitch but still needed to continue to do her Bath & Body Works job full-time. Vicky took on a big workload for six months to carry both of her assignments. What made her project even harder was that her boss didn't allocate additional resources to her for the pitch work.

"I had to rely on the relationships I had built to get things done," Vicky told me. "I continually had to convince myself that I could rise above the lack of resources and put together a great pitch."

When the time came for Vicky to make her presentation, the representatives from Disney told her the proposal was exactly what they wanted. They awarded Gryphon the business and Vicky was promoted to General Manager of the new venture. Her boss told her later he was surprised when she asked to take over the pitch. "I never thought of you as a leader," he said. "I had pegged you as a good soldier, not one who had a vision of your own."

By asking for the Disney project, Vicky turned her manager's impression of her on end. Clearly he wouldn't have given her the assignment if she hadn't approached him, asking for it. That type of scenario will play out over and over in your career if you make the decision to ask for what you want.

Women tend not to ask for what they want. That's what drove Linda Babcock and Sara Laschever, authors of *Ask For It: How Women Can Use Negotiation to Get What They Really Want,*[1] to research women-specific negotiating challenges and strategies. They found that even young women who claim they are good at negotiating and asking for what they want actually do not negotiate as much as men. In fact, the gap in the frequency that young men and women negotiate is about the same as the gap of that between older men and women.

Women are not only less likely to negotiate, they also have trouble when they try. Those who adopt the male model of negotiating come off as demanding. Their attempts crash stereotypes of the selfless female concerned more with others' needs than their own. Once again, women run into difficulty when they force someone else's style. Babcock and Laschever wrote *Ask For It* to give women a guide to successfully negotiate in an authentic style that will not alienate others. It advocates a "relentlessly pleasant" attitude that will keep the dialogue from becoming adversarial. The authors stress a win/win approach and at the same time give you tips to achieve top dollar, or top assignment, or whatever it is you're after.

This chapter will discuss some of the principles of negotiating, but because the topic is important enough for many aspects of your life, I would also urge you to read a book on negotiating. *Ask For It* is among the best women-specific books. I also recommend *Negotiation Genius*[2] by Deepak Malhotra and Max Bazerman, which clearly explains negotiation basics and details key factors that are relevant to both genders.

Choosing not to negotiate, or negotiating without using the best methods, could literally cost you millions of dollars over a lifetime. In *Ask For It*, Babcock and Laschever detail an example where two individuals with a starting salary each of $35,000 negotiate raises each year. One aims higher and achieves a 4.3% annual increase and the other receives a 2.7% raise annually. By age 65, had the higher earning individual invested his extra pay at 3% a year, he would have saved an extra $2,120,730. Those figures make a compelling argument for negotiating at the very beginning of your career.

Considerations Before You Ask

Let's say your boss has given you new responsibilities that will be a boon for your career but will require longer hours and more travel; one positive and two negatives in your mind. You are willing to take on the new work but you would like a pay increase to compensate for your new level of responsibility.

Before you approach your manager you need to **understand the environment.** In this example, that means you need to determine your value, or the fair compensation due to you. Executive recruiters, colleagues, industry contacts, and salary websites (e.g., payscale.com, salaryexpert.com, monster.com, indeed.com, salary.com, and careerbuilder.com) are all resources you can tap. Often the best sources are colleagues, even though you may feel uncomfortable asking them. But you'll be surprised how much information some of your associates will tell you about their pay or others'. If you can't bring yourself to ask, then pose a less direct question like "If you were me, how much would you ask for?" Your colleague's answer will not necessarily reflect his actual salary, but it can start a conversation about why he thinks that number is appropriate. When you determine the salary or raise that will reflect your value, stick with that number and don't reduce it because you can get by with less.

You also need to **understand the perspective of the person you are negotiating with,** including the factors and constraints that will affect her decision. Is she the primary decision maker or does she have to appeal to others? Will giving you a raise impact the pool of allocable income for others? What are her goals regarding her unit and how does your role help her establish those goals?

Understanding the other person's frame of reference makes the entire negotiation run more smoothly. It allows the conversation to **focus on interests rather than positions.** Defending your position can make you appear intractable and unwilling to consider the other party's concerns. But finding common ground through stating each other's interests will enable the discussion to proceed. So it would be wise to start the conversation in our example by telling your boss that you would like to help her develop the new initiative and that you're excited about the attention that it will give your unit within the firm. Begin to talk about "our" and "we," referencing your shared business goals to help her understand you have common interests. Your boss and you both want you to increase your responsibility. The conversation becomes a joint session on how each of you can do that.

And importantly, **aim high when you ask for what you want.** Negotiating theory proves that it is unlikely you will receive what you ask for, so request more than you have determined is your target amount. If your boss accepts the bigger amount you proposed, there's a good chance you undervalued yourself. You could have possibly received more.

As long as you remain **relentlessly pleasant and likable,** asking for more will not alienate you. What annoys those on the other side of the table is when a negotiator develops a position without acknowledging the other's interests, or when she is indignant if she doesn't receive as much as she hoped for. But if you remain friendly and positive, you will likely increase your reputation in the eyes of your negotiating opponent. That's a hard concept for women especially to understand, but I can attest to its truth. I was negotiating a contract for a job once and asked for much more than my future employer had anticipated. I could tell he was frustrated but certainly didn't think worse of me when he stated, "Damn it, Terri, that's why I want to hire you, so you can use your negotiating skills for us."

NOTE TO FILE: 

- Negotiate as hard for yourself as you would for someone else's benefit.
- You can ask for almost anything, as long as you have a smile on your face.
- Negotiating skills are among the most useful abilities a leader can possess.

Compensation

Learning how to advocate for myself for pay didn't come naturally to me. I came from a Navy family where salaries aren't negotiable. But when I started to work on Wall Street I learned that everyone cares about their year-end bonus. Even though I wasn't raised in a family that focused on income as a measure of achievement, I liked the competitive practice of shooting for top dollar. I decided pretty quickly that I would work harder than anyone else and I would get paid more. But I soon learned it doesn't work that way.

Self-Advocate for Your Pay

The fall after I joined my firm, I was offered a "high-profile" project for the office of the CEO. That sounded like a sexy enough assignment to me. Excited about my new role, I reported for duty to the associate in charge. Turns out, I was selected for the assignment because I was relatively new and didn't know the killer reputation of the associate. He had been known to chew up and spit out analysts in the past and was attempting the same routine with me. Hours were late (even by investment banking standards), praise was scant, and criticism was plentiful. And that was when he liked my work.

After a few months of that torture, I ran into another analyst from the other side of the floor who was one year ahead of me. Never one to mince words, he stared at me and said, "You look awful."

"Gee, thanks, John, nice to see you too," I shot back.

"I mean . . . have you slept at all this month?" he asked.

Then I told him about the high-profile project I was on and added that at least it's over soon and I'm sure I will get a good bonus because of it.

"Why?" John asked.

"Why? What do you mean, why?" I snapped, particularly annoyed that it wasn't obvious to him. Long hours, high profile, duh?

"Like, what makes it high profile? What are you doing? Have you met with the CEO?"

Well, actually, I hadn't met with the CEO or anyone other than my project associate. I crunched numbers and gave them to him, I told John. And to answer his question about what I was doing, I explained that I was analyzing expense and overhead numbers by department. After I finished describing how I had spent my time over the last three months, I realized that there really wasn't anything high profile about my project. But at least

I had worked hard for a notoriously difficult associate and was sure to be rewarded for that.

But when John asked the next set of questions, I began to suspect that my reward might be at risk too.

"Have you talked with the associate about your performance or discussed what he'll tell your manager about you? How about your manager, have you been keeping her up to date?"

"Wait . . . was I supposed to do that? Crap!"

I spent the next half an hour talking to John and learning some of the best lessons of my career. I had made mistakes accepting the project and not advocating for myself, which we'll address later, but this section is about compensation so we'll cover that topic now. What did I do wrong and what should I have done instead?

I assumed the associate would tell my manager I was doing a great job. My mistake was assuming anything. First of all, how did I know I was doing a great job? I had figured since the associate wasn't yelling at me, he was happy with what I was producing. When it comes to your performance-related pay or performance-related promotion or performance-related anything, you can't assume; you have to find out where you stand. Even if you know without a doubt that your manager loves 100% of what you do (unlikely for any of us), you need to sit down with him and have him tell you that. So, I should have met with my associate to discuss my performance and, assuming it was as I expected, ask him if he would advocate for me to my manager. I shouldn't have come out of his office until I knew exactly what he was prepared to do on my behalf.

That approach may sound bold to some, but it is your project supervisor's responsibility to advocate for you. I would not have been asking him to do anything that he shouldn't already have been planning to do. But supervisors need to be prompted and reminded of what you have accomplished.

I also should have been visiting often with my manager, the one who had the biggest input on my bonus. She needed to know that I cared about my pay, or she wouldn't care about my pay. It was my responsibility to make sure she knew what I was doing, how hard I was working (without sounding whiney), and the quality of work I was producing. I should have talked to her about my upcoming bonus and asked if I would be receiving a top payout because my contribution was significant. If I had done my homework and had an idea of what the range of bonuses would be, I could have supplied her with a figure, reflecting what I thought was appropriate. But sadly, I didn't do any of that. By the time I had my conversation with John, it was too late. Bonuses had been set.

Despite my lesson in self-advocacy, I was still surprised during a meeting I had several years later, sitting on the other side of the compensation table.

I was meeting with my boss to determine the bonuses for the vice presidents in our group for the year. My manager asked for my input, but I'm sure he had already made up his mind on everyone's compensation. When he ran through the numbers of two of the vice presidents, I thought he had the figures mixed up.

"But Emily has better reviews across the board than Matthew," I reminded my manager.

"I know," he said, "but Emily won't complain and Matthew will create an uproar. There are limited funds for the bonus pool. I've got to take it from someone."

My boss considered Emily complacent so she lost out in compensation. She didn't need to give the impression she would be a jerk, but she needed my manager to know that she was aware of her value and expected her bonus to be at the top of her peer group. She should have had that conversation before bonuses were set and elicited support from my manager and confirmation of his intention to fight for her. Adopting Matthew's contentious attitude is never a good long-term plan, but certainly Emily should have shown more concern than she did. ***Like all things in your career, if you don't ask for it, you won't get it.***

Even though the previous stories were about annual bonuses, you can apply the same principles to requests for raises. Do your research, understand your value, and let your manager know you understand your value. As a side note, unless you will have to leave the company as a result of financial need, avoid referring to that need. Managers are sympathetic but prefer to compensate based on value, not financial circumstances.

Overcoming Excuses About Your Compensation

So what happens if you get shut down? In the course of a salary discussion, it's very likely that your manager will tell you what a great job you have done and then begin to tell you the bad news. "Our group had a great year! Unfortunately the company's performance was terrible, so no one in our group will receive a raise." Or, "Our firm had the best year ever and you were a top performer! But our group as a whole didn't do so well so unfortunately, you won't receive a raise." Or, the ever popular, "Our company, our group, and you in particular had a fantastic year! Unfortunately, management is worried that next year is going to be tough and they want to be conservative with payouts, so your compensation will have to stay flat." Superiors are somehow always able to blame other parts of the company or other senior executives when you don't get what you deserve.

Don't let them off easy. There are always questions you can ask. Are others receiving additional compensation over last year's levels? If so, will I receive extra compensation as well? Find out as much as you can about the pay system and the division of pay so that you can discuss your compensation effectively. If more than one person is responsible for your compensation, talk to as many individuals involved as possible. Even if your company performed poorly, if you can argue that you contributed disproportionately to any company success, you may be rewarded for your performance, even in a bad year. My friend Jack, who had an outstanding history of negotiating his own compensation, achieved a significant bonus for the group he led, even during a recession year.

If you don't receive the raise you requested for performance reasons, what do you do to set yourself up for the future? You can tie your future improvement to compensation increases. Your manager is telling you that you don't warrant a raise because you failed to perform x, y, and z. So ask him if he'll agree to grant you the raise if you achieve x, y and z by the same time next year, then check in with him periodically during the year to make sure you are on track from his perspective and continue to fix any issues he might have.

New Job Pay Negotiations

When making a job switch, the same rules apply. A 26-year-old accountant named Jessica asked me recently if I thought she should negotiate an offer she had just been made by a prospective employer. She said it was a 16% increase over her current salary, which was "more than fair" and that frankly, she would take a 1% increase just to get out of her current stressful environment. She added sheepishly though that, even still, she knows a man would probably negotiate.

So what should Jessica do? You know the correct answer is that she *should* negotiate, but why? If the salary is "more than fair" then why should she negotiate when it would just add stress to her life? She's paid appropriately and she can get on with it. But wait . . . there is conflicting information. Jessica also stated that she knows a man would negotiate. So does she really think the offer is "more than fair" or not? What's fair is what anyone with her same skill set is able to negotiate. If some random man could negotiate more than 16%, the market rate is more than 16%. So yes, Jessica should negotiate. Perhaps she should just ask herself next time: What would a man do?

Generally most going-in salaries are negotiable, except for some post-college and post-graduate school entry-level positions. If your prospective employer won't move on the salary number, you may be able to negotiate some other aspect of the total compensation package such as the moving allowance, length of vacation, or severance terms. Even if you're pretty certain you can't improve your package, it doesn't hurt to ask. Your employer will realize you have solid negotiating skills and respect you more for it.

Compensation is an area where women have traditionally lagged behind men[3] for the same work. In 2012, women were earning 77% of what men were making doing the same job. Surprisingly, that pay gap starts one year out of college, with women earning just 82% of their male counterparts. As your personal endeavor to try to change that statistic, you need to be aware of your value to your organization. **If you do not demonstrate concern for how much the organization values you, the organization will not value you.**

Entry-level compensation and subsequent pay raises have more impact than many understand. If you join a company at a specific level, your compensation increases will all be based upon whatever your current pay is at the time. Even if you discover that a peer who has identical responsibilities to you is receiving 30% more, your manager may be unable to raise your salary beyond a 5% cap that year. You may never catch up to your peer's **market** compensation. Company policy often limits increases to a specific percentage, regardless of perceived value of the employee. And potentially more damaging, hiring companies often ask potential employees their last salary level and peg their offer to that number.

OK, enough about money. This chapter isn't just about asking for money, it's about asking for projects, asking for promotions, **asking for whatever you want!**

NOTE TO FILE: 

- Make sure you know when pay decisions will be made so you don't miss the opportunity to discuss your interests with your manager.
- When negotiating a new employment offer, understand all of your benefits so that you may barter between pay, vacation, and other items.

Projects

The Wall Street Journal sponsored an Executive Task Force[4] in 2011 with 200 leaders in government, business, and education to come up with an action plan for how each of these groups can promote women's progress in the professional workplace. One recommendation out of the gathering was for companies to "Take risks on high-potential women by rotating them through different positions and giving them exposure to senior leadership."

These leaders realize that women need exposure, responsibility, and opportunities for building skills through their projects. Yet managers don't offer those opportunities as often as you need them to. You have to ask for the assignments that allow you to meet leaders across the company. You should **request the ugly jobs** that will challenge you but will also help you build your skills, or the projects that will **solve company problems** and highlight your achievements.

Even if you think your boss knows you want certain types of assignments, you should specifically ask for the projects you want. Managers make assumptions about their employees' goals, and unfortunately women's are often misinterpreted. I had a conversation once about staffing a deal with a colleague who told me the man in his group would be a better fit than the woman. He said the man was more suited for the project because it involved travel and the woman had two small children. I told him she might be interested despite the travel. Later I told her to go ask for the project if she wanted it. Your boss won't do a good job of stepping into your high heels and figuring out what you want if you don't tell him what you want.

Which Projects Should You Ask For?

Some projects will be obvious high-flyers that will be great for your resume and reputation. But if you're not sure whether an assignment, or even a new position in another area of your company, would help your career, ask the following questions:

- How much exposure to key corporate executives will it give me?
- Will it help me build a relationship with a potential mentor?
- Will it add to my skill base?
- Will it develop high-quality business for the company?
- Will it help me develop repeat business with a client?
- How much revenue/market share will it create?
- What is the downside risk?
- Does it solve a problem for my boss or my company?

It's also important to understand the success criteria at your organization when you choose assignments. Each organization has its own ruler for measuring success. It could be the lawyer who brings in the highest profile cases, the technology expert who crafts the most creative solution, the banker who generates the most revenue, or the entertainment agent who attracts the biggest celebrities. Determine the factors that your boss will be able to judge you by.

And although you can ask for any assignment, you have to be careful about turning one down. You may be turning down a project to get a better career-enhancing one but come off as someone who's not a team player. Sometimes when you want the good project, you need to take on the unexciting one at the same time.

You also need to make sure you have developed a great relationship with your manager so that he wants to give you the good assignments. A young woman recently told me she kept asking for better assignments but didn't get them. I asked her to describe her relationship with her boss, how often she saw him during the day, and how frequently she spoke to him about anything other than business. As she was answering me, she realized that she rarely talked to him except to receive or hand in work. She never had lunch with him or stopped by to ask about his projects or his family. Her peers in the group, who seemed to work on better deals, acted more like friends of his. She realized pretty quickly that she needed to develop her relationship with her boss first and better assignments would likely follow.

Make a Solid Case When You Ask for a Project

Janet Piller, Chief Administrative Officer of an international development institution, thought she might want to switch into a different department at her organization. She thought working with client countries in another group sounded more exciting than the job she held in her own department. Janet figured if she could work on a project in the other department, she'd be able to determine if she wanted to make a switch. But she wasn't sure if she was qualified for the work, so she started talking to as many people as she could about the different role. From conversations with friends, colleagues, and other contacts, she learned the skills that were needed. Janet discovered that some of the skills she'd gained at her previous organization would be useful in the other group. She then approached her boss to ask if she could take on a project outside of his area. Her request included a plan describing how she would get her work completed with minimal extra support. Janet told her boss that she had someone who would back her up in every aspect of her work. "I made it easy for him to say yes," she told me.

Janet then approached the manager in the other department with her idea. She remembered the skills her contacts had told her she needed for the new job and described her abilities as they related to those skills. She had also learned which units needed help and targeted her discussion toward those areas. "The manager was a little skeptical," Janet told me. "He wasn't sure whether I had the right background." But she convinced him to take a chance. She started with a small project and wrote up the project with extra care and detail. The manager, surprised and pleased by the quality of Janet's work, put her on bigger projects. She took on assignments in Ghana, Rwanda, and Cambodia.

After completing several projects in the other department, Janet determined that the job wasn't as glamorous as she had thought. She decided not to move but felt good about having vetted the role before making a big career change.

Janet's experience illustrates the right way to get involved in a project outside of her group. She talked to as many people as she could about the role and the skills needed to fulfill it. When she appealed to the manager, Janet was able to highlight the appropriate skills for the job and appear as a possible solution to existing problems. And she presented the opportunity for herself as a seamless occurrence for her boss.

NOTE TO FILE: 

- Projects allow potential new managers to check out your abilities.
- Sometimes you will want to select projects to develop relationships with specific managers.

Promotion

When I made the switch from a smaller investment bank to Merrill Lynch, it was important to me not to lose ground when I made the shift within the industry. All of my classmates from business school were now "third-year" associates, and I wanted my new employer to hire me at the same level. Entering as a third-year associate, I would be promoted to vice president along with the rest of my class of business school students at the firm. So I joined my new company feeling good about having negotiated my title.

Yet a year later when the VP promotion list came out, I wasn't on it. It hadn't occurred to me to make sure I was in line for the title. Since I hadn't mentioned the promotion to my boss, I was certain he had decided to postpone promoting me to reduce my share of the overall group bonus pool. As an officer, I would have required a larger share. I approached him to discuss the issue and he awkwardly apologized, stating that the promotion had slipped his mind. Directly after our conversation though, he went through the necessary procedures to have me added to the list.

Even when you believe you are in line for promotion, you need to confirm the timing with your manager. In some cases your manager will have suggestions for things you need to do to make the list. A boss I had a few years later at Merrill Lynch knew my promotion goals and told me I needed to gain exposure around the firm in order to achieve them. At the highest levels, senior managers from all areas will have influence on promotions, not just those from within your group.

Get Known

Senior officers influence your pay and promotion, and they aren't always the senior officers who you know well. So it pays to develop your profile outside of your immediate work group. If there is a particular promotion committee at your company, try to find out who is on it. Ask your boss to assign you to projects that involve some of these individuals or seek opportunities yourself, as long as your boss approves. If you can't identify the promotion committee members, just try to create opportunities to get together with senior executives around your sphere of work. It isn't always easy to take the first step but generally, no one else is going to do it for you.

Or you might be lucky like me and have a manager who tries to help you. My boss suggested I call his boss and ask him to lunch, solely for the purpose of building my rapport with firm leaders. He wanted to put me in line for promotion to managing director and knew I needed to gain visibility in the firm. A closer relationship with leaders up my chain of command was the first step.

If your boss doesn't facilitate the connections for you, you should inform him when you meet with anyone up his chain of command, unless you had a prior relationship with that individual. If you worked with his boss in a previous group, it would be natural to get together with him. Otherwise, let him know that you met since his boss will probably mention it. You don't want him to think you have some sinister agenda.

The senior people at your company are known not only within the company but by most of their competitors and potential clients in the industry. Even at a junior level, you can begin to raise your profile in your industry. One way to do this is to volunteer to speak at industry conferences. Even a junior professional with a little industry knowledge and a bit of finesse can add value in a presentation.

Take the Lead

It's always important to remind yourself that no one cares more about you in your organization than *you*. Not your boss, not your mentor, not your sponsor. *You* need to communicate with your boss and other senior officers in order to develop your career goals. Have the appropriate conversations and tell your superiors what you want. Just make sure you're prepared, professional, and pleasant, and you will gain tremendous ground.

Now that you've learned some important things to do and not to do during a negotiation, you should feel good about the mandate proposed in this section. By following a few tips, such as: stay positive, be likable, talk about interests not positions, aim high, and make sure you ask for what you want, I hope you will now feel more inclined to take on negotiating challenges.

Women are the historical hunter-gatherer-bargain shoppers of the world. Centuries of practice not paying full price for things has transformed us into excellent negotiators. All we need to do is to let those negotiating skills have an outlet in the office. The commodity is different this time: it's you. So make sure you receive your full value.

Chapter 8: Damage Control

Don't you worry about me. I'll always come out on top.

—Pippi Longstocking

The division's numbers showed that once again, Mia's team generated more networking systems sales than any of her manager's six other units. She also had the best employee retention record in the division. Mia's manager had scheduled her to meet with him this afternoon and she hoped he was planning to offer her a promotion. She could use some good news; two weeks ago Mia found out that she had breast cancer and would have to undergo surgery, radiation, and chemotherapy. She tried not to think about it too much and had distracted herself pretty well by focusing on her family and job.

When Mia walked into her manager's office she noticed that the VP, Human Resources was there too. Before she could process what that meant, her boss began to talk. "Mia, we're so sorry about your current health situation. But I need someone who can work 24/7; I brought you here to take the business to the next level, and I know what breast cancer requires to recover—both my sisters and my mother had it. My sister actually had a mental breakdown from it and has never recovered. I know you think you're a superwoman, but you can't do what I need you to do and fight it.

Anyway, best of luck to you. As you know, we are in the middle of cutbacks and I am going to have to lay you off." At this point, the VP of Human Resources addressed Mia with a strange mix of compassion and disbelief on her face. She obviously knew about the layoff, but Mia guessed she didn't anticipate Mia's boss would deliver the message the way he did.

"Of course you will want to hire a lawyer," the VP said.

Mia never anticipated that she would be a target for layoffs. It was pretty clear to her, and apparently to the HR officer in the room, that her boss was tying her dismissal to her recent cancer diagnosis, which she knew was illegal. The courts agreed with her and she received a payment from her former employer. Mia, a true survivor on both fronts, shouldn't have had to suffer that injustice at work. Yet at times, people don't play by the rules. Her boss had tunnel vision regarding his goals and how to achieve them and decided that Mia's illness excluded her from his plan.

When Bad Things Happen to Good People

You might have assumed that the story above occurred in the 1970s or 1980s, when companies had not evolved as much; but it happened in 2014. Despite an improved workplace by most measures, managers can still surprise us with their behavior. Often we don't have control over these circumstances, but sometimes we have options to improve our fate. The following are some situations that can occur to anyone in the office and potential solutions describing how to deal with them.

Toxic Boss Issues

The story in Chapter 4 about my friend Kathryn with the threatened boss is one type of problem that can occur within the employee/manager relationship, but there are many more. You could have a manager who doesn't like you for no other reason than you remind him of someone else. Or maybe something about the pitch of your voice sets him off. You may never know what he doesn't like about you. Maybe it's not that he dislikes you, it's that he has favorites and you're not one of them. Remember, the familiarity principle tells us that the more time you spend with someone, the more they tend to like you. As difficult as it may be, try to let your boss get to know you better. He'll also be more likely to tell you what it is that you can do to improve your relationship. At the very least, if he knows you better, he probably won't care so much about the sound of your voice.

On the other hand, you might struggle with a boss who likes you a little too much and doesn't want to lose you. He may rely on you for support so that he can fulfill his role and fears that others will spot his weaknesses if you leave. The problem you face in that situation is a manager who will be unlikely to promote you much outside of your group. His needs may delay your progress to upper levels. If you suspect that situation may be playing out for you, it will be more important than ever to cast your net wide. Continue to ask for assignments where you can work with senior managers outside your group, despite your boss's reticence. Become aware of opportunities in other groups and realize that your advancement will rely more than ever on your own initiative.

Another tricky situation is when a manager tags you with a certain shortcoming. Oftentimes, despite a subordinate's success in overcoming identified problems, her boss may be slow to change his view. Human nature makes it hard for people to alter their perceptions, so you may just need to persevere if your manager demonstrates that tendency. Just keep working hard to combat the problem and eventually he will acknowledge and appreciate your effort.

Political Casualties

At times, the office mirrors political parties competing for election or warring factions vying for victory. But at work, the battlefield can be much more subtle. Generally, leaders try to position themselves for advancement, and their team members become associated with their successes and failures. If an executive is chosen for a top position, she will often bring her posse with her, elevating team members so they can continue to help support her. If she isn't promoted and instead passed over for a management peer, one of two things can happen: she may continue to prosper at the company, or her newly promoted peer may consider her a rival who never helped him gain stature at the company. In the uglier political scenarios like this, a leader and perhaps her entire team will be marginalized in a less important role. In fiercely competitive situations, she, along with some or all of her people, may be let go.

Whether you're a leader or a protégé of one, it's best to try to stay friendly with rivals and their teams so you can avoid any fallout if your side loses a turf battle. Even if your team leader falls out of favor, developing other strong senior relationships could help you escape any backlash you might otherwise experience.

Sometimes though, political maneuvering is hard to thwart. Renée LaBran, a partner with Rustic Canyon/Fontis Partners private equity firm, worked at the Los Angeles Times earlier in her career. After several years at the paper, a new CEO was brought in who quickly made many changes in the organization. After the dust settled, Renée was covering many of the duties of an open SVP position, but still held the title of vice president. She and her colleagues all assumed she would be promoted to the SVP position. But one of Renée's peers, also a VP, proposed a new organization plan to the CEO that would enhance the VP's role and eliminate the SVP position that everyone had anticipated Renée would assume. The CEO decided to adopt the VP's plan, causing Renée to report to a peer who had recently joined the paper.

She spent close to a year in that frustrating role considering new options. Fortunately, her luck changed. A top executive from Times Mirror, the paper's parent company, asked Renée to help him start an investing group. In an earlier role at her company, Renee had formed a close bond with the executive and since that time had continued to develop the relationship. While it was a tough path to get there, ultimately, Renée landed in a great position that marked the beginning of a successful investing career.

Renée didn't anticipate her peer's actions so she assumed she would be promoted to the SVP spot that she was functionally fulfilling. Nonetheless, it's always a good strategy to begin to develop a relationship with the decision makers as early and thoroughly as you can. And if an organizational change is likely to occur, it's especially important to present your ideas to your manager sooner rather than later.

You Become a Scapegoat

Major corporate disasters, like BP's Gulf Coast oil spill of 2010 or General Motors' massive recall in 2014, require management to respond quickly and publicly. In such high-profile mishaps, companies take steps to fix the problem, avoid the recurrence of a similar problem, and publicize the termination of those employees associated with the problem. All these actions are necessary from a PR standpoint, especially the punishment of people deemed responsible. The public wants to see justice done; they need to believe that the guilty will suffer. Even corporate mistakes that don't reach the public eye often yield the same response by management. People have a natural desire to pin blame when things don't go as planned. In the case of the lower-profile situations (where public relations isn't a factor), workers play the blame game for two reasons. First, they fundamentally want to determine the cause and take steps to make sure the issue doesn't recur, and second, they want to distance themselves from the mistake. The best way for employees to provide that distance is to incriminate others. They become scared and point fingers; that's how innocent professionals become scapegoats.

If you are ever in that situation, the best defense is communication. Be proactive about describing your involvement and recruiting others to back you up before too much misinformation spreads around the office. Even still, sometimes the criticism is hard to deflect. A friend of mine is a marketing VP at a personal products company. She discovered that before she joined her company, her administrative assistant began skimming company funds from petty cash accounts each month. The admin continued this activity for five years (one of which occurred when she was reporting to my friend), before managers in the finance department discovered the theft. Although my friend wasn't at the company for most of the time the fraud happened, she was blamed for lack of oversight as the company prepared a suit against her former admin. Yet the VP had done nothing wrong and wasn't in a position to uncover the criminal activity. The originators of the criticism were actually the employees in the finance department, the ones responsible for not catching the fraud. They decided to point fingers to take the heat off themselves.

NOTE TO FILE: 

- The stronger and more extensive your network, the better chance you have of shielding yourself from bad luck at the office.

The Repair and Recovery Mission

There may be times when you aren't a scapegoat at all because you are actually responsible for a big mistake. Or maybe you have developed a history of smaller performance issues that threaten your career.

The solution is not to hide; you need to talk to your boss. Make sure he understands that you will work to overcome your lack of judgment, your analytical weakness, or whatever your perceived shortcoming happens to be. Make sure to check back with him frequently for his feedback and suggestions. And if you can mend whatever problem occurred, take steps to do so. Remember, it will take some time for your total redemption, but be patient. Managers may have long memories, but most of them love to see their employees succeed.

Dania, a manager at a wholesale wine distributor, told me about her employee, Elizabeth, who she didn't think was going to survive long-term at her company. Elizabeth hadn't improved her sales numbers in 24 months when Dania sat down with her to review her performance. When she asked Elizabeth why she hadn't expanded her client base, the young salesperson told her she thought she was making progress with each account, but when she asked for the order, they turned her down. "That shouldn't stop you," Dania instructed her. "The sale begins when the customer says 'No.'"

Elizabeth had been doing everything right up until the time she asked for the order. When she did, her clients tested her and she didn't respond appropriately. They wanted to see if the price would move or what special terms they could get. They were used to being aggressively sold to by their distributors and as a matter of course turned them down initially. After Dania explained this, she watched Elizabeth over the next few months bring in sales as she never had before. "I give advice to direct reports all the time," Dania told me. "Some of them act on it and some of them don't. It was great to see Elizabeth take the challenge and really improve her performance."

Professional Frustration

Today's young professionals have job-hopped more than past generations. The media attributes this wanderlust to a variety of influences, but job dissatisfaction is at the core. Most of the factors influencing job satisfaction aren't too surprising: working conditions, workload and stress, recognition and responsibility, promotion and financial rewards, co-worker respect, and one's relationship with supervisors.

More thought-provoking is a study[1] by the University of Singapore, which found that the tendency to hate your job could be genetic. The article states that "People with a certain type of dopamine receptor gene, which has been tied to risk-taking, weak impulse control, and attention deficit disorder, tend to be less satisfied with their jobs." My non-academic interpretation is a little different: Those are the people who should be day traders on the New York Stock Exchange, reality TV adventure seekers, or serial entrepreneurs. They're just bored easily.

That tendency has been reported to be a characteristic of today's young professionals as well. Although there is always a lot to learn when you start a career, it's hard to jump from a fast-moving, multi-digital, multi-tasking world to one where you're assigned entry-level tasks from a manager who possibly knows less than you about aspects of social marketing.

Part of the problem may be overblown expectations. Graduates hope to find their *dream job* upon graduation and, when landing it, are often disappointed that it's not as glamorous as recruiters or even Hollywood makes it out to be. Or, they don't secure their dream job and have to accept a position that they rank as second tier. As a result, many of these new professionals are less than 100% emotionally committed to their jobs when they launch their careers. One fourth-year college student I spoke with recently hadn't even started working but asked how soon she would be able to switch jobs within an industry and how she should go about it.

Even if you don't like your job or can't stand your boss or your commute, as long as you are gaining important skills for the career you want, it's probably worthwhile to stick around for a bit. Sometimes you just have to pay your dues. After you've persevered enough to learn the skills you need, for perhaps a year or even more, you can start looking, listening, and talking to the appropriate professionals about a change if that's still what you want. One of those professionals may be your boss, so make sure you've kept up a good front.

It's generally easier to look internally first if you want to stay within your industry. Moving within your company will give you the advantage of starting a new job in a place where you're already respected. Push to work in areas at your company where you will gain the kind of experience that is particularly demanded in the rest of the industry.

A shift outside of your company into a new field can be difficult. If you are making a change, you may need to start at a more junior level compared to your most recent position. You also may need additional training or even an advanced degree to help you land a job in your next career.

If you have gained some identifiable skills, testing the waters for outside opportunities can be a healthy way to refocus your energy on your own job. When I was at Merrill Lynch, I interviewed for a position outside of the firm that I wasn't really interested in, but during the process, I gained a sense of control over my destiny. I realized I had options for my career that gave me more flexibility. That realization gave me confidence and prompted me to discuss career ambitions and goals with my manager.

The interviews also inspired me to openly discuss compensation issues with my boss since I gained a sense for my true market value. These discussions gave me perspective on my professional value in the industry and available alternatives should I want to access them in the future. Lastly, the discussions gave me a contact in the industry that I could call later in my career if the opportunity for a change were more appropriate.

There may be a time in your career when you decide that you are ready for a change. Either you have ultimately determined that you don't want to stay at your job, company, or industry or you've fallen out of favor and can't seem to regain ground at your organization. Then it's time to leave. Of course there's another reason to leave, and that's when you're fired.

Game Over

Marie Claire magazine recently interviewed Mika Brzezinski, co-host of MSNBC's *Morning Joe*. In the interview Brzezinski talks about the tears she shed after getting fired by CBS in 2006 and the job she took afterwards as a freelance reporter at MSNBC at a tenth of her previous salary. Even though she took the job because "it was work," it became the springboard for her highly successful post at *Morning Joe*. There are plenty of stories like Brzezinski's. An average of 55,000 people in the U.S. are laid off or fired every day.[2] And many of them will rise to better positions in their new companies, especially if their termination is due to a company-wide layoff.

Layoffs occur when your organization, the industry it is in, or for that matter, the entire world economy is experiencing a contraction, and workforce reductions are necessary for the company's own health and stability. Being fired for these reasons won't feel good either but at least you won't be alone. And, you can blame your situation on your stinkin' company.

Although ranting and raving would be *SO* much more satisfying, try to stay even-keeled when your boss terminates you. Despite the circumstances, your boss may be willing to give you a good reference when prospective employers call. Although bosses are seemingly inhuman at times, they generally dislike firing employees. They'll likely feel guilty, whether it was their decision or not. As a result, they genuinely may wish to help you in your job search. Therefore, either at the time of the layoff or in a later meeting, ask your boss to agree to act as a reference for you. Discuss the evaluation that he will give when prospective employers call him. Come to an agreement with him regarding the words he will use to explain the conditions of your termination as well as other information he volunteers about you. Offer sound bites for him to use if you feel he'll need help creating a strong reference. Here's an example of that type of conversation:

"Bryce, you always said I came up with creative solutions and was very effective with customers. Can you highlight those skill sets in your referrals? You could mention the re-branding concept I created for Newco Electronics."

Soon after you are laid off you should try to reconnect with your former colleagues. They could easily be called as references without your knowledge. They will also often be the best sources for job opportunities in the future. And remember to maintain your former professional relationships after you begin working at a new job. This advice applies whether you are terminated or you leave voluntarily. You can be helpful to former colleagues, and they to you, throughout your careers. But if you contact ex-colleagues only when you're looking for work, they'll be less inclined to want to help you.

Lastly, you do have a right to negotiate your departure package. It will vary depending on whether your termination was based upon an individual termination or a mass layoff. You are protected by federal laws that cover employee benefit plans and discrimination violations. Generally, regardless of whether you are let go individually or en masse, your organization will offer you a financial package at the time of your termination. This package will have been prepared by the Human Resources department and cover certain future job search–related expenses, health benefits, and compensation. You may accept the package or negotiate for improved benefits. These packages are often negotiated and generally both parties arrive at a mutually acceptable agreement. Don't be concerned that initiating a reasonable negotiation will hamper your relationship with your employer. As long as you remain unemotional and logical, you can generally expect to reach a settlement with no hard feelings.

When you do begin negotiating your exit package, you should be familiar with your rights as agreed to when you joined the company. A friend of mine avoided being taken advantage of recently because she understood her employment rights. When her manager called her into his office, he tried to sound upbeat. "Don't worry; we'll give you a couple months of salary." She then reminded him that her benefits package guaranteed twelve months of severance pay upon termination.

If you can't agree on mutually acceptable terms with your employer, you may decline the package and initiate legal proceedings to attempt to gain an enhanced settlement. In that event, keep in mind that you probably won't have an employer reference for your next job, or worse, industry employers will hear about the lawsuit and think that you're a potential hiring risk. You may still decide that legal action is the right path for you. You just need to ensure that you understand the potential negative consequences.

NOTE TO FILE: 

- It's tough to be unemotional when you've just been fired. Take a few days to clear your head before you jump into discussions with your employer.
- As hard as it may be, try not to sound bitter when you reconnect with your colleagues or when you interview for your new job.

Chapter 9: *Start Your Search Right*

It's our challenges and obstacles that give us layers of depth and make us interesting. Are they fun when they happen? No. But they are what make us unique.

—Ellen DeGeneres

After losing her brother to leukemia, Mary McLaughlin focused her energy on fundraising. Mary wanted more than anything to assist in curing the disease that took her brother's life. Her family developed a foundation that contributes to the Leukemia & Lymphoma Society, and she helped organize large fundraising projects involving fellow high school students and members of her community.

When Mary graduated from high school, she enrolled in Christopher Newport University in southeast Virginia. When she was there she discovered, though, that going to a small, relatively unknown liberal arts school created challenges when she was looking for a summer job. And there was one job that she wanted in particular, a White House Internship. She wasn't a political science, government, or international studies major and didn't have a recognizable school to gain her any points on her application, but she pursued it anyway.

"I spent more time on that application than I did on any of my college essays," Mary told me. "I wanted that internship so badly; everything I had went into it." She described the passion she had for the cause that had consumed her during high school. And she tied her past experience into her desire to give back to her community as an intern. The White House recruiters liked what she wrote. After a phone interview, Mary was selected as one of 125 summer interns out of 6,000 applicants for President Obama's first year in office.

A few years later Mary graduated but had not secured a full-time job. She specifically wanted to work for the Bill & Melinda Gates Foundation and decided it was better to graduate without a job than with one she didn't want. Mary told everyone she knew that she wanted to work at the Gates Foundation and eventually she found a friend of a friend of a friend who worked there and arranged to meet him for coffee. This Gates professional advised Mary to look elsewhere and said that an entry-level position wasn't the right job for her. But he did pass her name on to a manager looking for an assistant. The manager called her for an interview and then offered her a job.

With a profile that was unlikely to grab much attention, Mary did a lot of things right to gain a highly competitive internship and end up in an organization that many not-for-profit professionals consider their dream workplace. She took a great deal of effort filling out her internship application, conveying the passion she had in her past experiences, and projecting how she could offer that same commitment as an intern. She networked to find a connection to the Gates Foundation job she wanted, and when she found a contact, set up a meeting to talk to him. She weighed his advice but made her own decision that pursuing the job was still the right path for her. And most importantly, she never gave up.

Mary knew exactly what she wanted to do in high school, college, and at the start of her career. But many of us aren't sure which path will be best for us. For those just starting their careers or those deciding to change directions, the first step in finding a job is deciding what you want to do.

Starting Fresh

One of the best ways to find out what type of job interests you is to take a self-assessment. These evaluations also home in on what you do well and what you value in a work environment. Good self-assessments for professionals determine your interests, abilities, and values. Some of these assessments are based upon the six **Holland Themes,**[1] or personality characteristics, developed by psychologist John Holland in the late 1950s. Holland-based assessments categorize individuals by their combination and relative strength of these characteristics. Because jobs and work environments often reflect these themes, individuals are more likely to thrive if their personality patterns are aligned with the work situation. The results of these assessments highlight your dominant themes and suggest an array of fields and positions that fit with your type of personality.

Three high-quality assessments that you can self-administer are iStartStrong[2] from the Strong Interest Inventory family of evaluations, Kudor Journey,[3] and Career Key.[4] The price per test ranges from $9.95 to $34.95.

For those who want to try a more informal assessment,[5] career advice website, TheMuse.com, recommends thinking about what day-to-day activities you particularly enjoy (such as speaking with others on the phone, writing, coaching others, building Excel models) and which activities you don't particularly like. It advises you to explore what sorts of careers involve a lot of the tasks you enjoy and to steer clear of those that require a lot of focus on the activities you find draining. You can also practice answering questions like "My coworkers and friends always say I'm great at _________ because _________" or "If I had a free day that had to be spent 'working' on something, I'd do ________ because ________."

Are You Qualified?

After you have determined the types of jobs you want to pursue, it's time to begin networking, writing resumes, tailoring cover letters, and interviewing for those types of positions. You'll start to see opportunities and you'll gauge whether you're interested and qualified. But you should understand that research has proven that you will very likely be qualified for many more jobs than you think you are. And so will other women.

Women tend to believe that they are unsuited for jobs because they don't fulfill all of the qualifications listed. They lack confidence[6] about their abilities, intelligence, and their capabilities, which keeps them from competing for positions where they would be the best candidates. Men, on the other hand, have no problem applying for jobs and often believe they are the absolute best contender when in fact they have far fewer qualifications. So it's important to keep women's tendencies in mind when you are on a job search. Do you have 60% of the qualifications for a position you would love to hold? If so, go ahead and apply; otherwise someone less capable than you might be hired instead.

NOTE TO FILE: 

- Don't discount your individual abilities. You are probably much more qualified in each area than you give yourself credit for. Women tend to underrepresent the qualifications they possess.

Job Search Networking

When you start your job search, you can contact representatives from executive search firms, but generally they aren't particularly interested in junior professionals. Go ahead and meet with them; they may have a relevant opportunity and, if not, they could be a good source of industry and compensation information. But by far the richest source of opportunities for young professionals comes through networking. Referred employees account for about a quarter to a third of all hires in typical companies.[7]

Like the everyday networking you practiced before, you can call on business associates and contacts you've already developed. But there are a number of groups that you may not have accessed fully before your search, including your alumni network. Colleges will list by industry those who have graduated from their undergrad and graduate programs, so you can contact those in similar industries. Your former school club might also have an alumni list that will allow you to search for an even stronger connection.

Now's also the time to start out-of-the-box thinking about possible connections. Remember your lab partner's brother who worked for Amazon? You don't know him, but your classmate could give you an intro if you got in touch with her. Keep thinking; every day you will uncover more business connection opportunities that you hadn't considered in the past. A study[8] on Facebook usage determined that users are only 3.74 degrees (i.e., people in a chain of friends) away from every other user on the site. That means you're practically related to the CEOs of your target companies!

Networking Tools

Technology makes it easy for professionals to network. LinkedIn[9] has helped plenty of professionals and should be every job searcher's first source for connections. Human Resource departments use LinkedIn too, opting for the LinkedIn Recruiter tool, which allows managers to identify qualified professionals, even when those individuals are not specifically seeking jobs. Savvy LinkedIn users know to use first-tier and even second-tier connections to connect with targeted contacts. They also use LinkedIn Groups as an easier way to connect. The LinkedIn system provides fewer hurdles (such as target's e-mail required) to send a connection invitation to Group members so joining appropriate Groups is helpful.

Even Twitter has become a useful recruiting tool. I met Regina Chien, one of the best Millennial networkers I've encountered, through Twitter. She contacted me about a business opportunity and I worked with her on a project at her office in New York. Regina also found her current job through Twitter. One of her friends re-tweeted a job posting at Silicon Valley Bank that caught her eye. Regina then contacted an acquaintance in the tech space to see if that woman might know the person at SVB who posted the job. She did know him and made an introduction for Regina.

Industry-specific websites are also a great way to connect with other professional contacts. These sites allow interested members to learn from and connect with individuals in their particular lines of business. Many networking websites, originally created to counter a lack of opportunities for women professionals to connect, serve a female base. Women In Technology[10] specifically caters to females in tech and Ellevate,[11] originally a group for women on Wall Street, now attracts women in a wide range of businesses. Once you become a member, you can view profiles of other members and tap them for advice. Ellevate also facilitates local gatherings where its members can connect. It's sort of a women's LinkedIn where members are more likely to respond to inquiries because they're in the same "club." Websites like Levo League[12] and Lean In Circles[13] emphasize the creation of local groups of women getting together to share similar career interests. Levo League also provides a "Mentor" page, giving members opportunities to connect with industry leaders. Lean In helps facilitate women creating their own Circles on campus or near their homes and offices.

And of course, good old familial connections may provide the best connections, although some young professionals feel uncomfortable relying on family ties. I once interviewed a college student who hadn't put a summer job at a laboratory on her resume because her father helped her get the job. Many older professionals rely relentlessly on business relationships. But younger ones often think that taking advantage of a family-related contact feels like cheating. If you feel similarly, remember you may have had a hand getting in the door, but once in, your reputation is yours to lose. If you perform well, you will succeed; if you don't, it's unlikely your relative's friend will spend much energy covering for you. So please, take advantage of all types of connections, even those from your family.

One nifty by-product of the digital age is the e-introduction. Contacts can connect you almost effortlessly with another professional by copying both parties and introducing you via e-mail. These introductions work well because the two copied parties can go forward from there, with the implicit blessing of the common friend. The practice also tacitly obligates the two connected parties to interact. In fact, if one of your connections suggests that he will contact his colleague, leaving you to contact that individual afterwards, you might want to suggest he e-introduce you both instead. You'll be more likely to get follow-through from his associate.

The Informational Interview

Informational interviews are meetings between company professionals and job seekers who want to find out more about the organization or the industry but aren't interviewing for a job. If the company doesn't have any openings, meeting with one of the executives is a great way to build your network of industry contacts. The meeting could lead to a referral, resume advice, interview tips, or even a job down the road. But, since searching for a job tends to bring out everyone's insecurities, it's not surprising that greener professionals might hesitate to set up informational interviews. The job seeker might believe that the executive doesn't want to spend time with him or will decline the meeting, thinking he is going to ask for a job.

But generally, senior officers are empathetic to young professionals asking for assistance. They want to help you—if you approach them correctly. So, half the battle is successfully asking for the meeting.

First, target the executive to meet. The person should be in a business unit, not human resources, because you will discuss business, the industry, and your career, not a job at the company. If you have a connection with an appropriate professional at the company, consider using it, even if that company representative is not the ideal executive. Sometimes, getting in the door is the biggest obstacle.

When you contact the executive, make it clear you are calling to ask for career guidance, not a job; no one wants to have to disappoint you if you ask for something they can't deliver. You can ask for an informational interview or just say you would like to take a few minutes of the officer's time for his advice. If your original contact with him is friendly, professional, and respectful and disassociated with a specific job at his company, he will most likely make the time to chat with you.

Once you sit down with this professional, take advantage of the time you have with him. Tell him your job search game plan and ask him his view on it. Does he have any suggestions for you on your resume or a view on whether your qualifications would match the type of job you are pursuing? Is there anyone he would suggest you contact in the industry that might be helpful to you? As usual, be flattering, not obsequious, and don't talk solely about yourself, but be sure to show interest in him and his career path. Plan to do all this in 15–30 minutes and yet appear charming, talented, and brilliant. You ought to be able to pull that off, right? Who knows, perhaps if you do, a job may suddenly appear.

NOTE TO FILE: 

- Just like after a regular interview, send a quick thank-you e-mail to your company connection.

The Right Resume

The best way to think about a resume is to consider it from the standpoint of the recruiter. After an average six seconds looking at each applicant's submission, she makes a decision as to which pile to put it in. The resumes that don't receive even that much time are the ones that visually make her work too hard. They might not have enough white space or lack boldfaced headers to help distinguish sections. With the remaining resumes that have earned their full six seconds, she'll focus on the applicant's name, current and previous employers, job titles, starting dates, and education. She then looks for words that match the skills needed for available jobs. Here's where her review can balloon to an entire third of a minute. If your skills match her requirements and you have demonstrated those skills through achievements relevant to her company, she will gaze a little longer. And if the combination of past employers, roles, skills, education, and achievements strikes her just right at that moment, or she's feeling good-natured due to her caramel macchiato high, she'll toss your resume in the preferred stack on her desk and you can advance to the interview stage.

Your goal is to get that recruiter's gaze to linger. You can do that by creating a crisp, sharp resume that accurately reflects your achievements and skills.

Writing Your Own vs. Using a Service

If you are pressed for time or want the confidence of knowing you have a professionally vetted document, you may want to hire a resume service. But unless you need to produce a resume quickly and don't have a prayer of being able to devote the time to it, I would suggest you take a stab at creating one before you make the decision to hire a writer. Regardless of whether you use a service or not, you will have to undergo the conceptual phase of putting together a resume. You should ask yourself the following questions: What do I want to convey about my capabilities? What relevant skills did I demonstrate in my work and volunteer experience?

What achievements should be included? A resume writer will ask you to tell her about your job with these questions in mind.

You may also want to use a service because you're just not happy with the draft that you produced. Your instincts are correct; if you don't like it, hirers probably won't either. But you might have options other than having a professional create a document for you. Many senior executives have spent a lot of time reviewing resumes and know what they like, which coincidentally is generally what everyone else likes. So if you have access to a friend, relative, or appropriate mentor who has significant hiring experience, ask them to take a look. They will have the advantage of knowing your personality and strengths better than anyone you can hire. If you take this route, try to get a few people to look at your resume, since they will each have different insights. You will really be ahead of the curve if you can snag a reviewer in the industry that you want to enter. She'll know the language, the roles, and the measures of success that all need to be considered when writing your resume.

If you do decide to use a resume service, make sure you pick the right one. The writer should have a recruiting background, either as a Human Resources officer, an executive recruiter, or a senior professional with significant hiring experience. And any good resume writer will also go through an exhaustive process of discussing your goals and employment history with you and will continue to rewrite until the two of you agree on how the paper reflects these elements. If the writer's description of the process doesn't involve that kind of communication or acknowledge the need for rewrites, he doesn't really understand how to create a winning resume. Finally, ask for a recent sample of the writer's work (not one that you can see on a website, which might reflect more effort than they normally exert). The sample should be a compelling description of the professional's experiences that you can easily understand.

If you're still in school, absolutely take advantage of the career office staffers who help students with their resumes. They're good, they're cheap (free if you don't count the thousands of dollars of tuition you've already paid), and they are familiar with entry-level resumes.

Important Elements of a Resume

The Look. With few exceptions, good resumes have a pretty standard look. Recruiters like to know where to look to gather all the information that is pertinent for their decision. Not surprisingly, top resume layouts haven't changed much in 25 years. And they're not hard to find. When I was at Dartmouth's Tuck School of Business, I used its suggested traditional block format style, which was almost identical to the layout offered at Harvard Business School. It was also just about the same as ones offered today by both of those institutions as well as Monster.com and a host of other reputable resume websites.

If you are a graphic artist, photographer, designer, videographer, or have a similar type of experience, you can exert much more freedom with your resume. But you still want to consider the hirer's time when you put your document together. Creative is cool, if the reader can figure out what you've done and where you've been. And the creativity standard is high when it comes to unusual resumes. If you designed an envelope that blossoms into a floral-laced resume for an online stationery company, the unfolding mechanics better work perfectly and the floral design must be top notch. You would be better off going traditional than using any low-quality design elements in your creative resume.

The majority of professional job seekers should select more traditional formats by looking at several samples of others in your industry. You can find these online, at your college, or through friends in the industry. Look for clean examples that show some combination of short paragraphs and bullet points that will work with your experiences. Templates may be tempting but try to avoid using them. They are generally not perfect forms and can be difficult to alter.

White Is the New Black. One consideration to keep in mind over the course of your entire career is *Don't Fear the White Space.* If you're a new college grad, you may be ecstatic to hear that what you perceived as a lack of experience is really aesthetically pleasing. The message is really for professionals who have accumulated a bit of experience and want to explain every bit of it to their potential employer. Recruiters don't like to be overwhelmed when they look at a resume. Some of them find looking at blocky, give-my-eyes-a-break resumes so stressful or, more likely, annoying that they push them off to the pile you don't want them to be in. To that end, leave enough white space between categories and make use of bullet points to break up blocks in paragraph form. Make sure margins are wide enough also, 1.25 inches on the sides and 1.0 inch on top and bottom. You can uniformly shrink the borders somewhat to fit more in, but don't size them down by more than 1/3 of those original dimensions or you'll produce a crowded look. And after you think you've finished your resume, compare it to some well-written samples and see if yours can match them white-for-white.

Less Is More. Rarely do professionals in the first eight years of their careers need to expand their resumes beyond one page. Recruiters may find such wordiness arrogant or, at the very least, rambling. There are exceptions to this rule, such as a technical expert who lists systems she's mastered or an academic who lists published research, but generally one and done seems to work best.

Be Bold and Other Formatting Tips. Use of bold, italics, and bullet points will help you define sections in your resume and make the page easier to read. The best fonts to use are the most basic ones, like Times New Roman, Courier, Garamond, or Arial and the font size should be set at 10, 11, or 12 point.

The Style. There are two basic styles of resumes, the *chronological* and the *functional.* A chronological resume shows your experience and education in a reverse timeline, letting the reviewer scan your most recent accomplishments first. A functional resume groups your achievements by skill set, not by employer or date. The appeal of the chronological style is straightforward; it's understandable to the reader and tells a story about the job seeker's professional and educational life. Some writers choose the functional resume because they lack experience in the specific industry they are pursuing but believe their skills are applicable. The functional resume can also do a good job at hiding lapses in employment. But as it turns out, the world is filled with functional resume haters. They don't fully trust the writer, thinking he may be trying to hide something, and they get frustrated trying to parse through work history. Since many of these critics are hirers, I say scrap the functional and embrace the chronological. It's best to avoid annoying the people you want to impress.

The chronological resume should unfold, almost like a story, with the reader following your journey from one milestone to the next. And just as the reader does in a book, he expects a certain organization to help him uncover your story. He anticipates certain sections within the resume that will tell him what he needs to know about the candidate. These sections include the heading, the qualifications profile, education, and experience. Other optional elements include skills, licenses, publications, and interests.

The Heading. The heading includes your name, address, e-mail, and contact number. Just make sure you use your personal contact information, not any attached to your employer. And if your e-mail account reflects your boy-band preferences or distinctive body parts, instead of your name, hop on Google and create a name-based g-mail account. Some applicants include their social media addresses on their resumes. If you plan to work in a social media–intensive position in marketing or advertising, these additions can be helpful for employers going the next step at your candidacy. And a LinkedIn profile that includes publications, industry blogs, skills, registrations, or licenses can help you include information that won't fit in your resume. But if there is any chance that 100% of the material found on your sites will be viewed unfavorably by a potential employer, better leave it off.

The Qualifications Profile. This section is a relatively new entrant on the resume scene but can be a critical way to separate you from the rest of the pack. The profile sits right below the heading and relays your most important achievements and skills for the job you're seeking. It appears in paragraph or bullet point form. If you're looking for one type of job or similar jobs within one industry, then you'll be good to go with one resume and profile statement. But if you are looking into two or more different types of careers, prepare different resumes, each with profiles that reflect the skills needed for that type of job.

Although the profile is considered optional by many recruiters, I love it, especially for young professionals who have a variety of internships, summer jobs, or club officer and volunteer experience applicable to project work they may face in future jobs. They can describe their qualifications from all those experiences in one descriptive statement. For instance, take a look at the following qualifications profile:

> *Marketing professional with proven record of developing strategic marketing solutions. Experience in online and traditional marketing, search engine optimization, video content marketing, and digital content development. Demonstrated achievement in communicating with all levels of organization and effectively developing client relationships.*

This profile is for Kaila, a 26-year-old digital marketing professional. In putting together her profile she made a few key decisions. She opted to highlight an important but minor part of her current role, *developing strategic marketing solutions*, to cast herself more appropriately for the higher-level job she is seeking. Kaila also took the tact of describing her most distinguishing talents. She has a big personality and is unusually strong at networking across the company and with her group's customers. Since effective communication is critical for success in marketing, and ease with clients shows future management potential, Kaila highlighted the talents that would be the greatest asset to her future employer.

What if you are a college senior attempting to write a resume but don't have much experience to profile? You can eliminate a profile from your draft or you can get creative. You don't absolutely need a profile, and without a couple years of work experience behind you, you might be better off leaving it out. But if you do have applicable experience, even if it's from a club or volunteer role, you can integrate it into your qualifications profile. Here's an example of Molly's qualifications profile, incorporating her three years as sorority treasurer/fundraising chair:

- Three years' financial and fundraising experience in nonprofit organization
- Expertise in developing monthly income and balance sheet statements and analyzing cost reductions; proficient in Excel, QuickBooks, SAS, STATA, PowerPoint, Word
- Successful record of managing fundraising projects
- Experience recruiting, training, and motivating volunteers

Molly is able to describe her analytical, fundraising, and managerial talents up front, which will attract employers in the financial industry, her targeted field.

Some profiles open up with a compound adjective describing the writer such as a "results-driven" technology manager or "achievement-oriented" executive. But these self-described fancy modifiers don't really tell us much. Who doesn't think they're results-driven or achievement-oriented? "Proven" or "experienced" tells us that the writer has been around the block a few times, which is generally a good thing when applying for jobs requiring developed skills. Even "design-focused" could be descriptive if you are a marketing manager with a specific record in design-based improvements. It wouldn't be a helpful adjective, however, for industrial designers; we would hope they are design-focused.

The Objective. The objective is another optional addition to the resume, but today there are more detractors than fans. Most recruiters are primarily interested in quickly assessing what you bring to the table, not what you're seeking. I've even read of some hirers who are so annoyed with the objective statement that they toss out any resume with one included. The best approach is to leave your objective out of your resume but include a statement in your cover letter that explains why you are seeking that specific job. Your message will be more targeted and can show more passion for your choice than a resume would allow you.

Education. Education, like the rest of the information in your resume, should appear in reverse chronological order, with college first (including study abroad, thesis title, and any relevant courses of study) and high school second. The high school information can be excluded after you complete the first few years of college. Check with your school's career office to see if there are any specific conventions that recent graduates of your school follow. One college senior I spoke with said her career office advised her to include her GPA and SAT/ACT scores only if she achieved a minimum threshold. Other schools advocate including those figures solely for consulting and finance jobs, whose recruiters require them. Find out what hirers are expecting to see from graduates of your college.

For current students and recent grads, the education section appears ahead of the experience section on your resume. But after your first job, you can switch the order of them so experience is above education. At that time, you can also eliminate the grade point average and testing score figures.

Experience. In the recruiting world, experience is king. But that doesn't mean you need to have worked at a high-profile company to grab a recruiter's attention. You can make your experience jump off the page by highlighting accomplishments and achievements, rather than duties and responsibilities. Review every sentence you write to confirm that **you aren't merely describing your role, you are conveying your successes.** Use figures throughout to quantify contributions you made, positively impacting your group or your company. Include hard data when possible: revenues generated, costs reduced, time saved, processes improved, customer satisfaction increased. Resumes with quantifiable achievements will catch the attention of the recruiter much more readily than those without. If possible, even show figures describing your accomplishments in your club activities and volunteer jobs.

A summer job as a museum tour guide/intern can reveal much more about a candidate's skills when it goes from this:

> *Processed contracts for and supervised evening events, gave tours, and handled petty cash.*

To this:

> *Advised museum special event clients and finalized event contracts. Selected by manager as only intern to supervise 15-member summer staff during evening events and coordinate client requests with catering staff. Conducted four tours daily of up to 50-person adult and student groups. Collected, audited, and deposited cash receipts from entrance, tour, and event fees.*

The revised description introduces elements of client interaction, managerial skill, public speaking, cash management, productivity, and trustworthiness. Each of these new elements highlights successes, which should be your central focus in crafting your resume. If part of a description sounds like a duty, then either change it to make it read like an achievement, or get rid of it.

One way to highlight accomplishments is to put powerful verbs behind them. Avoid words like *involved with* and *participated in.* Instead, opt for action words that transform you from a work voyeur to a catalyst of change. The museum intern didn't just *process* the contract, making her sound like a robot, she actually had to talk with the clients and clear up any questions that they had regarding the events. By using a more powerful verb, she goes from an order taker to a client advisor. In the Appendix, you will find Barnard College's Resume Action Verbs. Most universities and resume websites have similar lists of words, but I like Barnard's because it categorizes the words by the type of skills you're looking to emphasize.

Another thought to keep in mind while you craft your resume is to **design it for the job you want, not the job you have.** You do this by emphasizing the achievements in your past work experience that will be applicable to your targeted new job. A description of the type of job you want should give you a pretty good idea of the qualifications needed. Sometimes you have to dig deep to figure out how to best portray your experience for the job, but remember you can highlight past projects, even small ones, that may be relevant to prospective jobs, even though they didn't seem significant to your career at the time. You can also include volunteer jobs or part-time work. If in one of these positions you demonstrated, especially in a quantifiable way, a skill that is valuable to your target employer, by all means include it.

The job description should also be a starting point for incorporating *keywords* into your resume. Keywords are used by recruiters to cull through resumes electronically in *applicant tracking systems*. These systems identify keywords, generally from the job description, and screen on those words to produce a manageable number of resumes to review. Even if you know a human will take the first pass at your resume, using keywords makes sense, since the hirer will target resumes that reveal similar experience to that listed as a requirement in the job description.

Keywords relating to jobs in science, technology, engineering, and math (STEM) have appeared in an increasing number of resumes lately. For new graduates alone, there are over two times as many STEM jobs available and starting salaries are 26% higher[14] than for positions in non-STEM roles. Creating a STEMier resume, highlighting the analytical aspects of your past jobs and any STEM-related training you have received, or even courses you took in college, could help you get a job and increase your starting salary. A marketing professional I know wisely incorporated budgeting and data analysis language in the description of her role. It was a small part of her work but the reference caught the eye of a tech company representative, even though her job was in the fashion industry.

When I reviewed resumes for new college graduates at my investment bank, I realized that most 22-year-olds don't have jaw-dropping experience. I looked predominantly for three things: 1) Was the candidate motivated to work? 2) Was she smart? 3) Did she demonstrate an aptitude for analytical subjects? I would definitely prefer a smart, involved humanities major showing a proficiency in computer science and accounting than a middle-of-the-pack finance major with scattered activities, none of them too demanding.

Experience can appear in paragraph or bullet point form, or a combination of both. The short paragraph/bullet point combo for each job listed visually looks great if you have enough information to include for that format. That approach also allows you to use the paragraph to cite general accomplishments and the bullet points to drill down on specific achievements. Try to keep the paragraphs to three or four lines at the most and the bullet points to no more than five for the best visual impact.

Activities, Skills, Awards, and Interests. These headings can appear together or separately, or not at all. Make the decision based upon how much space you have and how important (to the reviewer, not to you) each of your additions to these categories is.

Activities appear more on student and recent grad resumes than professionals who have been out a few years. Often *Volunteer Activities* is a better heading for more established professionals. If an activity helps describe positive aspects of your character or illuminates a significant talent and you spend a good deal of time on it, you should consider including it. You don't have to feel that you need to rationalize how you spend your free time by adding a list of activities. So, whereas:

> *Member: Environmental Club, Outing Club, Technology Club*

won't be a worthy addition;

> *Organized and led first-ever 15-student team to successfully summit Mt. Ranier*

demonstrates leadership, management skills, and courage—all useful traits in the business world.

Activities should also avoid reference to your religion, political leaning, or ethnicity unless you are applying for a job where those affiliations are considered a plus, such as an intern at the Democratic National Convention.

Skills and Awards such as foreign language expertise, computer programming skills, and articles published should be included if they are relevant to the job you are targeting. Some resume advisors advocate leaving out the Interest section altogether, but I think an unusual interest can be a conversation starter. An interviewer may skip over "enjoy cooking," but may want to ask you about "Member of winning confectionery team, national cake decorating competition."

Other. Including "References Available Upon Request" takes up valuable space in your document so leave that out. If the employer wants references, he'll be sure to ask for them.

NOTE TO FILE: 

- Don't forget, first and foremost, your resume is a marketing document.
- Don't list responsibilities; describe achievements.

Online Applications

More and more companies are using online applications to narrow their list of potential hires. Human resource representatives who favor these applications believe they give a better opportunity to discern specific information about candidates and to compare potential hires against one another. You can use a lot of the information from your resume on the application, but you should also tailor your answers to the specific company and job description for which you're applying.

Tailoring a Cover Letter

When a job opportunity allows you to attach a cover letter to your resume, you've just increased your chance to score an interview. With a cover letter, you can highlight your unique talents, discuss your qualifications for the specific position, and let a little personality shine through. It also allows you to show a connection between your background and the job requirements that might not be obvious in your resume.

Do Your Homework

Before you begin to create the letter, research the company, the industry, and the particular position. The cover letter is really an exercise for you to connect the dots so that the hiring executive can learn how your interests, skills, and experience can benefit his company. If you understand how the target company fits within its industry and differs from competitors, you can demonstrate a level of interest that is far more compelling than a general comment about how much you love the company. You've taken the time to learn about the industry and the organization; you're interested and you can explain why.

To learn about a company, access the usual suspects—contacts you have at the company or in the industry, the company website, its LinkedIn page, and its Twitter account—and make sure you do a web search on the organization for recent news, discussions, and blogs featuring the company and its products. Job websites like Glassdoor[15] and Indeed[16] offer company information, interview questions, salary data, job openings, and company reviews written by past and present employees.

Another great way to get a snapshot of the company if it is publicly traded is by going to MSN Money[17] or Yahoo Finance.[18] Once there, enter the company's stock ticker symbol (you can find the ticker on the company website or by searching for it on the web). The company-specific page you land on will have stock price and financial performance data, recent news, lists of competitors, industry standing, and a wealth of other information. Even if you are applying for a position seemingly unrelated to finance, these sites will highlight useful information to help you understand the company's business. If you really want to get to know what's impacting the company, go to the company website, click on the "Investors" tab, or something sounding like that, and look for *quarterly earnings call presentations and webcasts.* The research analysts casting questions at the company financial officers each quarter drill down on any big business issues facing the company in the next several months.

The Format

For a professional look, follow a block or modified block style for the cover letter with approximately one-inch margins, 10- to 12-point font, and a conventional typeface such as Times New Roman, Arial, Courier, or Garamond. The letter length should be anywhere from one paragraph to 3/4 of a page. Much more than that and your efforts run the risk of being skimmed over by the reader. So unless you have a compelling reason to write more, and that reason is apparent to the recruiter in the first few paragraphs, keep your letter short and impactful. Whenever you can, put a real person's name in the salutation.

Pre-thinking the Letter

Before you start tapping on the keyboard, take a minute to do a little self-reflection. Begin by asking yourself why you're the best person for the job, not why your resume, experience, and education will or will not get you an interview.

Aileen Richards, Executive Vice President and Head of Human Resources at Mars Incorporated, says, "If young professionals were more self-aware, they would increase their job-searching success. I asked one candidate in an interview how she would describe her *style of influencing people,* and she was at a loss for words. I helped her out by pointing to the part of her resume where it stated that she was president of her on-campus a cappella group. She then told an impressive story about developing a consensus during a contentious period in the group when half of the historically all-woman club wanted to admit men and the other half didn't. She was a leader but hadn't reflected on why she was effective."

Aileen's observation regarding the value of self-awareness can be useful in crafting a cover letter, even before you have the opportunity to interview. Why have you been successful in the past? Why do you have a gut feel that you will nail the job if you can just have the opportunity? It may be your passion for the company or the industry, your work ethic, ability to lead, attention to detail, creativity, analytical skills, or a variety of other attributes. Whatever that talent or set of skills is, it makes you a **unique applicant** for the position you're seeking. You are different, but you need to determine how you are **unusually qualified** for the job. Once you understand how you are, you have to get the recruiter to understand as well. And she will, if you create a cover letter that conveys the insights you have about your specific talents. If you have relevant experience, you want to reference it, but your goal is not to reiterate achievements presented in your resume. Instead, **you want to create a letter that allows the recruiter to understand your talents well enough that he can easily see how you could succeed at his company.**

Creating a letter like that sounds like a tall order, especially when you adhere to your 7th-grade English teacher's advice to "Show, don't tell." So you can't come right out and say "I am a great leader," because, well, why should anyone believe you? And you'll sound a tad arrogant anyway. You need to tell a story that explains why you're a great leader, and you need to tie it back to the proposed job and the skills required for the job. If being a great leader isn't a skill set necessary for the job you're targeting, you've picked the wrong talent to address in your cover letter. Don't get confused with the skills required for a job you will be targeting in 10 years. Leadership is a great skill to have as a project leader on the Coca-Cola brand management team, but if you're 23, passion for the product, attention to detail, and strong interpersonal skills will be more valuable.

The Content

The letter, like any good piece of writing, will have an opening, a middle, and a closing. The opening should cite the job you are applying for and the company contact who referred you, if there is one. That reference alone may shift you to the *consider* pile.

The body of the letter is where you describe the qualities that make you a unique applicant for the job. Tell a story if it helps (and it is brief and on-point) or just describe a specific experience that was great preparation for the job. You can point to achievements in your resume but only if you can make them come to life in your letter. The reader will have the attached resume so you don't want to reiterate something she'll see anyway. And if the job is a stretch relative to your previous experience, you'll have to attack that issue straight on in the cover letter, or your resume may not be compelling enough.

The middle section of the letter should also talk about why you are interested in the job or the company. Conveying an authentic depiction of your interest is critical. The recruiter doesn't need to hear that his company is the largest in the industry (he knows that) or is the leader in the industry (he knows that, too). He is interested in why you specifically want to work for the company. If there's a story behind your interest, go ahead and share it. You might write, "I became a fan of Zazzy Co. five years ago when I first bought one of its products online. Since that time I have been so enamored with the products and so interested in Zazzy's different approach to retail, that I have read every bit of business news that has been printed on the company. I have also watched as Zazzy became what I would consider the most innovative company in its industry. When it created the Z-line of fabrics, bringing electronic technology into fashion goods for the first time, I knew this was a company I would like to work for."

If you don't have a compelling story as to why you have admired the company for years, write briefly about aspects of the company you find attractive, whether it's a specific type of job uniquely offered at the company or a teamwork culture that is different from others within its industry.

The closing can simply state how you will follow up. You can either ask the recipient to call you or state that you will call him within the following week. There's a good chance that even if you ask for a call back, you will have to follow up and call the recipient.

Remember too, while hirers respect humility and thoughtfulness, don't overdo it. I received an e-mail from a young professional interested in joining my consulting business. She wrote, "I know that this may be too much to ask but I was wondering whether I could take a half hour of your time, although I would understand that you may be tied up." The respect quotient in that letter was way over the top. Remember, you will be an asset to the prospective hirer's company. Plus, generally when you send a cover letter and resume, the executive receiving it is in a hiring mode. You may be doing her a favor.

Nailing the right tone is important too. At the end of the day, if the hirer thinks you're overconfident, insecure, immature or a host of other unattractive adjectives, there goes your chance for an interview. Somehow, you need to develop the right mix of confident-not-arrogant, qualified-not-begging, and overall mature, approachable, and interesting. But don't worry, you don't have to fret over each word as you write. Just write your letter with your voice, not the superhuman you would like to be, and go back and re-read it for tone. Pretend you're on the receiving end, not the initiating end, and ask yourself if you would like to be stuck sitting next to the letter writer on a 45-minute commute home from work. Not so much? Then you need to make the letter more engaging, less whatever-else-it-is.

Delivery

You might send a cover letter and resume through a mail service, in which case you should use matching paper stock for each document. But you will forward most of your documents to the reader through e-mail or submit them online through a hiring portal. When delivering through the web, make sure both documents are in PDF form, to avoid inadvertent word processing changes as they travel the internet. Although a cover letter is conventionally a formal document that can be attached to an e-mail along with your resume, if you know the recipient, you can choose to write the letter directly into the e-mail and use a more casual style. Regardless of your familiarity though, realize the e-mail will likely be sent to others whom you don't know within the organization. So starting the note with "Hey Claire, you were such a beast out-chugging those guys last night!" probably isn't a good idea. If you're not sure how casual your tone should be, write a quick, friendly e-mail referencing the cover letter and resume attachment and opt for a more businesslike tone in the documents.

Chapter 10: Interviewing for the Offer

Failure isn't an option. I've erased the word 'fear' from my vocabulary, and I think when you erase fear, you can't fail.

—Alicia Keys

My interviewing days stretched back to my work just out of college. After being at the firm for six months, I started interviewing college seniors who were looking for jobs like my own. Everyone I spoke to appeared to have done well in school and in their summer jobs. They were all friendly and nice. So I awarded most candidates top marks on their evaluation sheets. I realized eventually that I wasn't doing a good job of differentiating which candidate was better. So I started to ask the tough questions. I would challenge a comment a candidate made to see how he would respond. Or I would ask him a question about a class or a previous job that would allow me to assess his analytical ability. That small change to my interviewing technique significantly helped me differentiate the candidates. But I still tried to leave candidates with a good feeling about the firm, our group, and hopefully me.

Miles, a candidate I interviewed when I was a senior officer, had already been warned by the junior officers in my group that I might be his toughest interview that day. By the time he landed in my office, I knew everyone wanted to hire him, so I hoped to quickly confirm their opinion. Miles and I had an easy conversation until I asked how well he did in college. He awkwardly spilled out an account of two classes he bombed but described the situation that was interfering with his schoolwork at the time. After hearing the story, I decided Miles did a good job of rebounding from a bad situation and knew I wanted him to join our group.

We hired Miles the next day and he started work one week later, the day of my group's holiday dinner. I was surprised, but impressed, when our new junior hire grabbed a seat next to me at the table. Later that night he laughed as he told me his version of the interview. Miles said he was so nervous when he walked into my office that he began to sweat through to the back of his jacket. He strategically turned to hide his back each time I changed position in my chair. When I asked him about the one topic he had hoped to avoid in the interview, his stomach started to turn. Then at the end of the interview, Miles said he backed out of the office as he thanked me, ran out of the building, and threw up in the bushes.

While interviewers don't try to make you sick, they do try to determine if you're a good fit for the position. And if you are prepared, you can convey that you are. It's important that you respond confidently when the interviewer throws you a curve ball and make sure you get across the image you are trying to present. But to nail a job interview, you need to prepare.

Interview Questions

I was attending a birthday celebration recently when I watched one of the other guests make a high school senior sweat a bit. David Walker, head of corporate banking for Citibank in the U.K., asked Courtney how many colleges she was applying to. She said "just eight" but added that she had friends applying to 14 schools. "Writing that many essays would take forever," she said. "Plus, it adds up to a big expense since the applications average $60 each."

"And how big an expense would that be?" David asked.

Courtney, who was taking AP Calculus at the time, froze. She knew how to multiply 14 by 60 in her head but was so shocked by the question, her brain shut down. David witnessed her reaction and said, "Courtney, it's a good idea to always be prepared for a question like that. You never know who might offer you a summer job."

David was employing one of the finance industry's favorite interview techniques, but you can run into an analytical-based question in any field. Google has been posing the now famous *Google questions* for years now. When you Google "Google interview questions," 451 million entries appear. What David, Google recruiters, and everyone hiring want to do when they ask you to solve a problem is to determine if you can think on your feet. Generally your thought process is more important than getting the answer right. So if you are asked how many bagels your corner bagel store sells a year, you need to walk through your assumptions about bagel demand, seasonal variation, population of local market, impact of corporate function demand, etc. The interviewer doesn't know how many bagels the store sells and doesn't care, he just wants to hear you think the problem through.

Some questions are much easier but those tend to be the ones you have to prepare the hardest for. TheMuse.com offers four questions most likely to be asked in an interview: 1) What was your experience at your previous company like? 2) Why do you want to work here?

3) Why did you leave your previous job? 4) What do you know about our company?

I would add that almost every recruiter will ask you some form of "Tell me about yourself." That request allows you free reign to highlight the aspects of your experience, interests, and character that you want the hiring manager to focus on. But it's a much harder question than it seems. You should practice giving a two- or three-minute response. The ability to tell an interesting, structured story about yourself is a critical skill.

The Mock Interview

Interviewing is a skill like any other; you need to practice to be good at it. Before you begin the interviewing stage of your job search, practice the words you're going to say out loud, not just in your head. Ask friends, family, alumni, and career office representatives to give you mock interviews until you are comfortable answering whatever question gets thrown at you. A friend of mine practiced interviewing with her family. She said that in some ways, they were harder on her than the actual hiring manager. But then again, they weren't afraid to be brutally honest, whereas an interviewer might not pursue an area where he perceived a weakness. He may just make a negative judgment and the candidate could lose a job opportunity. As a result of the practice sessions, my friend gained comfort with answering difficult questions but also learned from her husband that she had a bad habit of scratching her nose during the mock interview. He said it was distracting. My friend had no idea she was touching her face and is much more aware now and careful with her hand movements when she interviews.

A graduate from my business school also figured out something she was doing wrong when she asked me to conduct a mock interview with her. She had been very successful interviewing between business school years but wasn't getting any traction during her second and final B-school year, a time when it really counted. She explained that she hadn't received an offer after her summer job because her project manager left the firm. After I heard her story, I could see how recruiters may not have been completely convinced that her project manager would have offered her a job in the first place, since she hadn't provided enough details. If I were a busy hirer, I would nod politely and tell the candidate we would get back to her. But since I was helping, not hiring, I pushed her on the topic and found out some important information. The project manager left the day before the group's officers met to select the summer associates who would receive full-time offers. The process included bankers endorsing their associates in an almost competitive round-table discussion. But no banker could say much about the MBA who had worked with an officer who was no longer there, so they decided not to give her an offer.

Then we honed her presentation so that she would preemptively offer the details that a recruiter would need in order to understand why she left her job without an offer. She would also relay that her former project manager offered to be a reference, adding validity to her story. What this student needed to do, but wasn't, was to **think like an interviewer.** An interviewer will make assumptions if you have a significant unexplained issue on your resume. Put yourself in his place and practice responding to the issue until you believe he will be satisfied with your explanation. You need to be brief, modest, and lack defensiveness when explaining any areas on your resume that the recruiter could perceive as a problem.

Inside the Interview

Of course when you arrive at your interview, first impressions are important. TheMuse.com also offers insight on how people perceive you when they first meet you.[1] Their impressions rely 55% on the way you dress, act, and walk through the door; 38% on the quality of your voice, grammar, and confidence; and 7% on the words you choose to say. You can certainly change the hiring professional's mind after you begin the interview, but it will be easier if you work on presenting the right initial image so you don't have to pull yourself out of a hole later on.

Once you begin the interview, try to cover experiences that you think will highlight your skills and knowledge. If your interviewer is asking you a question that doesn't allow you to bring those points out, try to guide him toward a discussion of them. Realize too that when you are giving an account of your experiences, describing them without discussing the challenges you have faced won't give the recruiter much to judge you by. He will want to know how you responded and what obstacles you had to overcome. You can also include stories that demonstrate humility and an ability to recover from mistakes. Often a hiring manager will learn more about you when you give an account of a failure that taught you a lesson. Own your mistakes; they have made you a wiser employee. The recruiter will be glad that you learned a lesson at someone else's expense, and you can bring your knowledge to your new position.

Be positive and upbeat even when you're talking about the reasons that you want to make a switch. Even if you are escaping from the worst work situation ever, you need to avoid piling criticism on your old work group. The interviewer really doesn't know your situation and may decide you're just a complainer. If you don't like your old group, maybe you won't like your new one. So when you describe your former job, *looking for new challenges* sounds better than *escaping from a lazy, sadistic boss.* And while you're being positive, make sure you are positive about yourself. Even if you don't have all the qualifications that you think you should have, don't apologize for your lack of . . . *whatever.* You may not have that skill, but you have so much more to offer, so let the recruiter focus on your positive attributes.

At the end of the day, your hiring manager wants to know if you can grow in your role at the company and ultimately manage people, win customers, and be graceful under pressure. My friend Rob had a second round of interviews at a company that set him up to meet with five professionals, one after another. When Rob walked into one of his last interviews of the day, the manager looked at his resume and began to rip it up. "This piece of paper is ****," he said. "Your background has nothing to do with the job you're interviewing for."

"I think it does," replied Rob calmly. "I'll explain to you why . . . ." Rob got the offer because he showed that he didn't get flustered and got the conversation back to discussing his fit for the job. Rob said, "I assume this guy did the same thing to everyone he interviewed. It was a sink or swim test."

Before the interview is over, make sure to ask a few questions yourself. The best inquiries will reflect a real understanding of the business. Maybe it will be a question about strategy going forward or about the company's position in the market. You can also ask about the hiring manager's impressions of the company and why he chose to pursue the career he did. The answers to the more personal questions should shed some light on the values of the people you might be working with. And make sure your questions don't sound canned and overly rehearsed. The best candidates pick up on what company professionals say and are able to form questions around those observations. Whatever you ask, just make sure "When will you make a selection?" is not your only question.

NOTE TO FILE: 

- When you're given a brainteaser-type question, think out loud to show the hirer your thought process.
- You can have all the skills and achievements in the world and the recruiter won't hire you if you're not a "fit." Try to make a personal connection during your interview. By the end of the meeting the hirer needs to conclude that you're likable and would work well in her group.

After the Interview

Send a thank-you e-mail but make it short and sweet. Three or four sentences are fine. The hiring officer will appreciate your acknowledging the time and effort she spent and will also expect you to express your interest in the company. But in most cases, that's all you need to write. The thank-you note is a courtesy, not another opportunity to sell, so don't make her have to spend time answering additional inquiries or reading an alternate answer to the question you blew in the interview (she was probably less interested in the answer than how you handled yourself after you messed up).

If you know you are one of a very few being interviewed for a position you can stray a little from the short format. Just make sure any reflection you offer is thoughtful and pertains to your previous conversation or the recruiter will think you're wasting his time.

Rejection Happens

Many of us move on quickly when we don't receive a job offer from a company. But a decline may be an opportunity for you to build a relationship or maybe even open a door to another opportunity. Regan was originally turned down for her job in the film industry. When she received the rejection, Regan wrote a *thank-you anyway* e-mail to her initial contact who had sent her resume to someone else in the organization. The original contact, who didn't know she had been rejected, called her up immediately and had her interview for another position where she was hired right away.

Even if you can't turn a rejection into an offer, you still might be able to build a relationship with a manager who interviewed you. If you had a good rapport in the interview, write him a thank-you note and tell him you would like to tap him for career advice down the road. Wait until you have a job so he doesn't think you're fishing for a position again. When you do reconnect, act like you would with any other outside contact. He then becomes a business connection whom you can draw on for advice, industry knowledge, or job search contacts in the future.

After the Offer

Whether you sensed it was coming or not, it feels awesome to get a job offer from a company where you would like to work. If you receive a few offers, you might have to do a little extra work to narrow your choices down. And if you still have questions about the company or group you would be joining, you can always ask to meet with your prospective colleagues again.

But whether you're holding one offer or several, you will have leverage negotiating your contract. In fact you may have more leverage now than you might have for some time at your present company. Once you receive an offer, the hirer, who spent a significant amount of time and effort determining that you were the best candidate, wants you to accept. So before you do, talk to your prospective employer about a few of the things outlined in the sections below.

Compensation. For more senior positions, you will negotiate compensation with your business contact at the hiring company. More junior candidates may need to have those discussions with the Human Resources department. If you're not sure who to go to, start with the business manager and he will direct you to HR if he's not able to negotiate. You should enter into those discussions if you believe the offer doesn't reflect the appropriate amount for the position or your value. If after negotiating you still feel like you deserve more, ask for a review before the standard period. An earlier review might speed up a salary increase or at least give you formal feedback before you might otherwise receive it.

In addition to your salary, find out the details of any incentive compensation or extra pay for performance bonuses that you would be eligible to earn. This type of payment could be commission tied to sales or an annual bonus. In either case, you need to find out as much as you can about how incentive compensation is awarded so you can understand how to maximize yours.

Moving Expenses. Even if everything you own can fit in the back of a car, it's worthwhile asking the Human Resources department about moving expenses. The cost of transporting household effects and your own travel expenses (including gas, mileage, and tolls if you're driving) are often covered. Your new company's plan may also cover your vehicle's transportation on a car carrier. Ask about house-hunting or apartment-seeking expenses, even if they are just day trips for you. You may also be entitled to reimbursement for flights, taxis, trains, subways, meals, hotels, and tipping costs.

If you need to sell or buy a home as a result of your new job, your company may agree to compensate you for a loss on your home or pick up your financing fees or closing costs on a new home. Also take a look at any contingencies tied to your moving costs. I moved to a different firm once after an 11-month stint at my prior job and received a letter that I had to reimburse my former company for my original moving expenses because I hadn't stayed at least 12 months at the company. Oops, I hadn't read the fine print! Fortunately, my old boss intervened for me and the company dropped the request.

Savings Plans, Insurance, and Health Benefits. Take the time to learn the details of the insurance plans offered by your company, and if you have any questions ask the HR professionals. You could spend more money than you need for insurance or healthcare for your family if you misinterpret the plans. Traditional savings programs at companies can also be worth investigating. 401(k) plans are almost always good investments, especially when your company matches your invested capital.

Employee Education. Ask the Human Resources representative how you can qualify for any internal training programs that the company offers and find out details on the tuition reimbursement terms for any outside programs. Will you be expected to complete any additional certifications or degrees on your own time or will the company grant you time off? And, as in the case of moving reimbursement, determine whether your reimbursable education cost obligates you to stay with the company a certain amount of time and charges a penalty if you leave early.

Vacation. Vacation length at bigger companies often can't be negotiated, but smaller, flexible companies might be willing to discuss additional vacation days to get you on board. In either event, make sure you understand the organization's policies. How many days will you receive each year? When will that amount increase? Are you allowed to roll over vacation or personal days from one calendar year to the next? You should also find out if you are eligible for *personal days* (days off that don't count against your vacation allotment) and if so, how many.

Work/Life Balance. Certain policies can be a revealing measure of your prospective company's attitudes toward its employees—especially its female employees. And while flex time, telecommuting guidelines, and savings plans might be unimportant to you now, they could have a big impact on your life later. Similarly, if parent leave policies don't impact you now, they may someday. In the U.S., under the Family Medical Leave Act, upon the birth or adoption of a child, men or women employed for at least 12 months by a business with a payroll of at least 50 people may take 12 unpaid weeks off and not lose his or her job. Some companies offer more than 12 weeks and some companies compensate the parent during the leave.

NOTE TO FILE:

- Read your employment documents and ask questions. The material may be dry, but it includes important information.

It Takes a Village—Thank Your Support Team

Once you have actually accepted a job, don't let too much time go by before you thank the many people who helped you in your search process. It's a courtesy to keep them up to date, but also realize that they really want to know what happened to you. You can send a blanket update e-mail to some but call those who were particularly helpful to you. You may want to take a few of them out to lunch, which they will appreciate as a show of gratitude without an agenda. So enjoy your new job, but don't forget the people who helped you get there.

Chapter 11: Work/Life Integration

Don't confuse having a career with having a life.

—Hillary Rodham Clinton

Sherri Oberg was at home one evening with her two toddlers during her husband's annual boys' golfing trip. She was having her house renovated, which made watching her children a challenge. They loved climbing over wood piles and wanted to touch the construction equipment and each of the tools on the floor. That night, Sherri, CEO of biotech company Acusphere, Inc., tried to keep her toddlers out of trouble while she crammed for her board of directors' meeting, scheduled for the following day. Her new venture capital partner would be at the meeting and she wanted to be on her game. "I had no doubt that my new partner would grill me on the numbers," Sherri told me.

She hadn't made much progress on her work when a storm passed overhead, dumping buckets of rain on the plastic sheets serving as the roof of her house. Unfortunately, the makeshift roof was no match for the nor'easter that was tearing through the Boston area. The plastic-sheeted roof blew off, the plaster in the center of the family room ceiling gave way, and torrents of water rushed into the room. Sherri quickly plucked her kids off the floor and planted them above flood level, then grabbed her photo albums and started rolling up rugs. After getting her toddlers to bed, she spent the rest of the night in triage mode, trying to save her possessions every time a new leak sprang through the damaged ceiling.

Sherri survived the deluge and the board's questions the next day, but the board meeting ran past the anticipated end time and she knew she would be late for a preschool meeting that evening. She grabbed her things, flew out of her building, and jumped in her car. As she began to pull away from the office, a disturbing image caught her attention: the gas gauge read empty. Sherri figured that if she stopped for fuel, she would miss the meeting altogether, so she took a chance and started driving. But right after she got on the Massachusetts Turnpike, her car ran out of gas. Sherri sat there trying to figure out her next move when, thankfully, a state trooper stopped and gave her enough gas to make it to the next station. She thanked the trooper and went straight to the preschool. When Sherri sat down at the meeting, adrenaline coursed through her body as if her veins were filled with coffee. She slowly began to relax a little. The only thing she had to do before she went home was to buy gas and a gallon of milk. After leaving the preschool, Sherri stopped at a gas station and started fueling the car. Then she headed toward the station's convenience store, where she tripped on the curb, ripped her hose, and tore open her knee. That last bit of bad luck tipped her over the edge; Sherri began to cry. "I never cry," she said, "but that was some 24 hours."

Every working mother will go through stressful periods and they'll figure out how to deal with them. Sherri realized she needed to share more of her responsibilities with her husband and get some additional outside help. She also made sure her husband's next boys' weekends didn't coincide with her board meetings!

Millennials and Their Careers

Young professionals now value their non-work time more than did workers in generations past. As a professional born in the Millennial Generation (between 1980 and 2000), you're different, partly because, even childless, you have much more to do than your predecessors ever had. You volunteer for community projects, participate in adult sports leagues, and become active in consciousness-raising activities.

The Benefits of Gaining Value at Your Organization Pre-Family

According to a PwC study,[1] Millennials have decided that they are unwilling to commit to making their work lives an exclusive priority, even with the promise of career rewards later on. PwC makes the case that some of the Millennials' attitudes have permeated the workplace, and now employees of all generations are beginning to believe lifestyle and flexibility play a bigger role in their lives. The study points out that "Millennials want more flexibility, the opportunity to shift hours—to start their work days later, for example, or put in time at night, if necessary. But so do non-Millennials, in equal numbers." And men are beginning to embrace flexibility for themselves and their partners as a necessity of family life.

So the paradigm is changing, let's hope in part because women are slowly making strides in penetrating the upper levels of corporations. How does all this affect the young professional woman working her way up the ladder? The change in values by employees and corporations allows women to have more stable platforms to succeed in their careers and home lives at the same time.

But if home/life priorities have seeped down to the youngest, childless levels in the workforce, women could possibly fare worse down the road when they attempt to gain the flexibility they need to work and care for their families at the same time. For example, let's say a 28-year-old woman is in a serious relationship and planning a family a few years down the road. She works in an industry that is more demanding than the ones most of her friends are in. She gets along well with her manager and teammates and is happy with her job except when she misses out on gatherings with her friends because of work, which happens often. Her manager approaches her one day and offers her a raise and promotion that would allow her to add to her skill base and manage more people. But the new position would require longer and more unpredictable hours as well as more travel. She loves to travel, but these trips would be to unexciting locations where her company's manufacturing plants are located. Today, many women in her position would be more likely than workers in previous generations to turn down the promotion in order to maintain the lifestyle they enjoy. But that decision could be one she regrets in the future.

Millennial women don't have the ability to look into their future, but those who want to start families down the road need to plan ahead as life will start to get a lot harder. And it gets worse . . . one of my colleagues warned me that "When you have your second child, you lose all the free time you thought you didn't have with the first child!" Your priorities will change too when you have children. Even though I loved going out at night and hanging with my friends when I was a young professional, I never had more of a desire to have free time than I did after I started a family.

Making the social and home/life sacrifices before you have children will set you up for a better post-child lifestyle. Your goal is to gain flexibility when you most need it in your career. You gain that flexibility by becoming valuable to your organization through the accumulation of skills. Maybe you have developed a unique talent for winning clients or positioning company brands. Whatever it is, accumulating that expertise takes time, and generally, the more senior you are in an organization the more value you provide.

Too many job changes can hamper a professional's ability to gain skills and experience, so women should think about the best way to integrate future family and career goals before they consider job switches. There are all sorts of reasons for these job changes, including opportunity, pay, promotion, lifestyle, work environment, company culture, and interest in social responsibility. But excessive job hopping can be a potential liability for women's ultimate work/life balance.

Job changes that add to your skill base and professional level will help you achieve the stature and reputation you need to be able to control aspects of your career when family demands multiply. And if any of the other factors that inspire you to move also mean that you will be miserable if you don't, you need to make the change. But building your reputation at your company, from gaining expertise to developing your network over time, will help you when you most need to control your job schedule and achieve more work flexibility. So think about the big picture when you make your plans. Will it be better to gain experience now and move to an elevated position in a year within your own firm rather than take a similar job today at a company where you're not well known? Consider that starting a new job might require a year to ramp up before you can operate at full productivity. Take into account your future desire for leverage when you determine the right moves for you today.

By the time Margot Rogers, Vice Chairman and Senior Advisor at the Parthenon Group, asked if she could work part-time, she had already shown her manager that she would do whatever was needed to get her job done, even if it required staying late or working from home after normal working hours. Margot's company had also begun to rely on her to mentor new employees and develop junior staff. And since she had been working at her company for several years, Margot had gained institutional knowledge that would have been hard to replace. When she asked to transfer to part-time work, she had become valuable enough that her managers wanted to accommodate her rather than lose her. Her organization even had to hire another individual to take up the slack but it was willing to, just so Margot would stay on in some capacity.

In addition to gaining flexibility, another benefit of pushing hard early in your career is being better qualified to offer consulting services. You may want to take on independent contract work or consult from your home when you leave your current situation.

You'll see later in the chapter, opting for that type of work can be an important path to maintaining your skills and network during phases of your career when you choose to work less.

Advanced Education

Although obtaining an advanced degree isn't feasible for every woman, you may speed your advancement if you do. Earning an MBA in particular translates to enhanced skill sets and provides you with the necessary credentials for moving up in an organization. Advanced business programs also teach a wide range of entrepreneurial skills that benefit graduates looking to start their own ventures. Today, approximately 60% of CEOs of S&P 500 companies hold advanced degrees.[2]

Only you can decide if the investment in a graduate program is right for you, but timing, once again, will have an impact on work/life issues. Those able to acquire advanced degrees before they require more job flexibility are likely to gain a greater amount of control when they need it because the degree will likely hasten their promotions. The credential and specialized business knowledge that comes with it may also make a woman's return to the workforce easier after taking a break.

Some of you who earn an advanced degree may decide not to return to work after leaving to care for your family. I asked Annette, an MBA who worked for several years before deciding to stay home, if she regretted taking the time and expense to earn an advanced business degree. "No," she answered. "The education and credential helped me with many of my volunteering roles including starting Cleveland's first Dutch school. I can't say I ever felt over-educated."

Sharing Your Time: Working With a Family

The Expert or middle management stage of a woman's career can be the most difficult in many ways and is the jumping-off point for many career women. At this time in their lives, women often gain more responsibility both at home and in the office; but the extra duties in the office don't always arrive with extra authority, making women feel less in control. This stage is also a time when women gear toward the leadership positions ahead of them by trying out different management styles, often with varying degrees of success.

Although some blame ambition on the attrition, statistics show that 47% of professionally qualified women see themselves as very ambitious when they start out their careers.[3] Yet only 16% of women hold senior corporate leadership positions in the United States.[4] Why the discrepancy? Structural biases in the workplace make it harder for women to advance, as do family pressures and society's view of men's and women's roles. Change is coming, but right now, it's coming in baby steps. Over a recent five-year period, the average percentage of women managers compared to total managers has increased in every industry in the U.S., but only by an average 2.7%.[5]

How Do Successful Women Manage a Career and Family?

Women who successfully manage their career and family life point to a few factors that have had the most influence. Those factors are quality childcare, appropriate division of home life responsibilities, and a feeling of contentment, pride, and control at the office. The impact of each of these influences and how to try to control them are described below.

Quality Childcare. Many women consider the quality of their childcare the most significant factor in their ability to maintain a challenging career as a mother. My own decision to start a home-based advisory business stemmed in part from a call I got one night from my daughters' ballet teacher. She told me that my new nanny must have left the baby in the car because she walked my two girls up the flight of stairs to the class without him. That same night I discovered that the baby Tylenol bottle that I had just bought was empty. My nanny had asked me earlier if she could give the baby some Tylenol if he was uncomfortable due to his teething. I hadn't expected she would empty the bottle in one day. I quickly called the doctor to make sure my son would be OK and then let my nanny go.

I was fortunate though to have had a fabulous experience with my first nanny Mary Theresa McFadden, who began working for me when my first child was born. She was my Mary Poppins who allowed me to feel completely comfortable at work. She taught me a lot about childcare, was beyond dependable, and to this day is beloved by my entire family. Women I know have had similar experiences with day-care options as well. To find out more about childcare issues, from a different perspective than you may have heard, I interviewed Mary Theresa.

Mary Theresa concluded from her many childcare experiences that women who don't feel confident with their dual roles are bound to worsen the childcare situation. Mary Theresa explained that "It's understandable that mothers become uncomfortable that someone else is spending possibly more time with their child than she is. I take care of the children and play with them, and the poor mother comes home exhausted, sometimes feeling like an outsider. But the ***children always know who the mother is,*** *and no one can replace her. What I've noticed is that if mothers feel insecure, they might send mixed signals to their children. They might cancel a punishment that I've given, or tell the children they don't have to clean up their toys after I had just told them they had to. These mothers want to win points with their child, and that's understandable, but doing it by overruling their caretaker will make their lives harder. The children begin to ignore my requests and rely more on their mother for care and discipline. They might even call their mother at work when they don't like what I've asked them to do. The mother then needs to focus much more on her children while she's at work and at home, and, as a result, both sides suffer. I've seen this happen time and time again."*

This situation can occur with part-time sitters and day-care providers as well. Women have enough struggles trying to manage career and home. They need to seek the childcare that's right for them, either in their home or at a day-care provider. Their entire work experience will be affected by how smoothly their childcare situation runs.

Family Responsibilities. One of my friends told me about her sister and brother-in-law who began to have arguments related to each one's responsibilities at home. She said it seemed to her that they had divided up the list of duties pretty equitably. But her sister complained that her husband "never did anything." "I can't just keep doing all his work and mine too," she said. "I'm exhausted and angry." When my friend talked to her brother-in-law, she began to understand the root of the problem.

"She's right. I don't do much. I tried to do everything we agreed upon but she complained about the way I did it. I either don't cook, clean, or care for the children the right way. She corrects me every time. At the office, when I'm given responsibility, I have authority. Here I have no authority. She wants me to do my share, the way she wants me to do it. So I gave up."

My friend, who was single at the time, said that was a life lesson for her. She remembered it years later, every time she thought her husband should be doing things differently. Sometimes, the bigger issue for women is not unwilling partners, it's holding on to too many responsibilities that they could relinquish. That's why families are traditionally led by partners, so partners can share the responsibilities and the joy that comes with raising their children. My friend Melinda had a deal with her husband. "You do poop, I'll do vomit," she said. "You really need to know your strengths and tolerances," she told me. "Unfortunately, I didn't think ahead to the many years of potty-trained, sick children."

You also have to know when it's time to contract out some of your duties. Jill Ker Conway, former President of Smith College and a board member of Merrill Lynch during my tenure there, emphasized that point in her convocation speech to my freshman class. She told the incoming class three things that most of us still remember. Jill stated that we were "women" not girls and shouldn't allow anyone to mistake us for the other. She advised those of us who would have partners in future years to take turns emphasizing each one's careers. And most memorable to many of us, she told us we were capable of great success and should hire housekeepers, so we could use our time in more creative ways.

Jill was ahead of her time. Although she never had children, she and her husband made sacrifices for each other when career opportunities arose. Her suggestion to rotate emphasis on each one's career doesn't work for every couple, but a surprising number of successful women have shifted the focus between careers with their partners at some point. As business managers and society become more willing to view women's and men's careers as equally valuable, let's hope opportunities like that will be available to more and more couples.

Lastly, remember that your choice of a lifelong partner, if you choose to have one, will be the most important decision of your life. It will also impact your career success dramatically. No woman is an island, and support from your partner, friends, and colleagues will help you achieve your goals.

Control Over Your Career. As mentioned earlier, you'll be much happier if you have some control over your work schedule once you start a family, and the best way to gain control of your schedule and gain flexibility is to become valuable to your organization. One way to gain that value is to become as senior in your organization as possible before you start your family, so you will be able to have that additional flexibility at the office when you need it. Realizing that there is a delicate balance between fertility and seniority, I respect anyone's decision to bear her children when she sees fit. I will say, though, life was a lot easier for me having children as a vice president, when I had already gained a reputation at my firm.

If you fill a role that would be hard to replace, you will have a greater ability to get what you want. But you have to ask, even when you think you don't have a shot at getting it. A classmate of mine turned down a promotion because it included more travel but discovered later that the woman who took the job didn't travel nearly as much as she thought the job required. The woman had been able to negotiate a compromise with her new boss, which my classmate hadn't realized would be possible when she first considered the job.

Another way to gain control is to set limits for yourself. When I had my first child, I decided to leave the office every night at 7 p.m., which made me the first of the 20 people in my department to leave. Since I had waited until I was relatively senior to have children, my manager knew I would complete my work no matter what time I left. Leaving at that time was a little rule I made for myself that I broke occasionally, but just having it made me feel more in control.

Another rule I made for myself was to never be away from home for more than two nights in a row. That one got broken too, but I was usually able to rationalize the exceptions in my mind (like leaving Sunday night doesn't count against my total because I saw my children all weekend). I remember having to make a trip to Hong Kong for a meeting that defied my two-day rule. I felt guilty when I told my four-year-old daughter that I would be gone for a few days and didn't know how she would react. Devon thought for a minute and said, "Mommy, will you wear that pretty pink sweater in the meeting so you can be beautiful?" Devon was more concerned about my fashion choices than my absence, which made me feel better about my trip. Her response also made me realize that my children were fine without me when my job called me away. Like many mothers, I was experiencing needless guilt when my work and home schedules collided.

One more note on making rules for yourself at work: You may feel you have so little control you can't even make a rule that you won't break frequently. If that's the case, institute a simple plan that you can reliably fulfill, to make you feel more on top of your work/home life balance. Maybe it's spending an extra 15 minutes on Wednesday mornings to have breakfast with your children before you leave for work or calling home every Tuesday after your son's karate class. Whatever it is, select something that fits into your routine, and make it a point to do it consistently.

The other rules or customs that working mothers find helpful are ones that ensure their priorities outside of work get attention. An Ernst & Young study[6] revealed that, in addition to guilt about not spending enough time with their children, working mothers feel most guilty that their house isn't clean, they're not doing enough to take care of themselves, and they aren't spending enough time with their partner. The women I interviewed who made traditions like date night or lunchtime exercise classes to respond to some of the limitations of their working mothers' schedules seemed to be able to cope with some of these stresses better.

All of these rules of course will change as your family grows and matures, but having certain guidelines or traditions related to your work and family will make you more comfortable bridging the gap between the two.

Career Hibernation. A few of the women I interviewed for this chapter talked about a convention that worked well for their careers and home life. They told me that during the first years of their children's lives they went from full-time to part-time work or took full-time positions that were not career-enhancing; those jobs were more like **career hibernation.** It wasn't full-on Mommy Track, because all of these women hoped to stay eligible for senior positions down the line. They just needed to take a career breather while they had young children.

Liz Lynch, currently a Senior Managing Director at Evercore, a financial advisory firm, was a Morgan Stanley banker when she asked to switch to a part-time role. "The job wasn't really advancing my career," Liz noted. "But it was the right job for me at the time. I was grateful the firm gave me the opportunity to work part-time at all. Four years later, I was asked to become the firm's Administrative Officer reporting to the President, which meant moving back to working full-time. Ideally, I would have stayed part-time for a couple more years, but the opportunity was hard to pass up; I took it and never regretted the decision. One year later, I transitioned to a new role as head of Human Resources.

"As I look back, I see just how much of a turning point it was when I asked to work part-time. Had they declined to let me make that move, I would have quit. When I returned to the workforce later I wouldn't have had the benefit of those terrific opportunities. Staying in the game was much more valuable than I realized."

Liz advises mothers today not to underestimate the value of a flexible workplace. "The best companies for working mothers are ones that allow you to switch from full-time to part-time and back to full-time without much of an interruption to your career. Those options are worth asking your HR department about when you plan to join a company or take maternity leave."

Stay in the Game When You Leave

Perhaps women of the Millennial Generation will plan better, but the Baby Boomer and Gen X women before them didn't position themselves well for re-entry after they left the workforce. Others didn't anticipate ever returning to work and when necessity or desire prompted them to begin a job search, they weren't prepared. As one woman I interviewed said, "I never planned to go back to work, but then again I never thought one day I would wake up and realize I had an alcoholic husband. I wish I had been prepared."

The demand is so great for women who want to return to the workforce, universities and business schools have rushed to serve that demographic. Businesses have even entered the field. A career re-entry strategy company, iRelaunch, provides conferences that offer strategies, tools, and connections to help professionals return to work.

The best plan for professional women today is to position themselves for re-entry to the workforce, **even if their intention is not to work again.** Attitudes and circumstances change. There's no loss in being prepared and deciding to stay at home but with no preparation, returning to the workforce can be a titanic task.

Since you may decide to return to work (and 55% career-oriented stay-at-home moms surveyed in the Ernst & Young study said they would like to), it pays off to try to gain as much seniority as you can before you leave. You will have a broader range of skills to offer once you try to return, thereby giving you a better shot at being re-employed at a higher level. You may also be more employable with your more defined set of skills and possibly a better age fit with the jobs you are seeking. Nicole, a mother who left the workforce in her late 20s and decided to go back when she was 39, said she really didn't know what she would do. "I'm tired of my friends telling me that I'm smart and I could do anything. Regardless of my potential, no one will hire me. I didn't establish myself enough earlier in my career to be able to market myself now."

You are also more likely to be able to offer consulting or contract services on a part-time basis from home if you have developed enough skills through your experiences at work. And the more experience you have before you take time off or transition to at-home consulting, the more valuable your services will be. For women, who are known to be less confident than men, feeling proud of what they have accomplished while they were in the workplace will carry over to their life after the office. Even if they never return, they will feel good about what they have achieved.

Maintain Your Relationships. The most important thing you can do to make your return to the workforce easier is to maintain your professional relationships. Even if you are sure you will not return to the same industry, you should keep up with your former colleagues and industry contacts. They respect you and can speak to your talents. They could be your strongest advocates at a later time when you're planning to return to work.

Carol Fishman Cohen, co-founder of iRelaunch and co-author of the career re-entry strategy book *Back on the Career Track,* takes this advice one step further: "When keeping in touch with colleagues, don't forget about people who were junior to you when you left, whether they reported to you, you mentored them, or they were just people you knew. Remember, while you are on a career break, they will be moving up. They may be in a position to open a door for you some day."

Yet many women make clean breaks when they off-ramp for maternity leave. Others stay in touch for a while but ultimately feel intrusive because they're always the initiators or they don't think their former colleagues will be interested in talking to them anymore. Your colleagues liked you before. You're really no different now. And yes, you are interesting, even though you may have spit-up on your face and pureed carrots in your hair. Call your old colleagues (just don't use Skype). And plan to meet face to face occasionally, too. That's what you would do with a friend and that's what you need to do with a work relationship.

When I was researching this chapter, some of the women I interviewed told me that it's really not feasible to stay connected to someone you worked with 10 years earlier, but I told them that's what I have done and it works. It hasn't always been easy, especially now that I live several hundred miles from Wall Street, but I still keep in touch with former associates by e-mail and phone, and try to connect in person when I'm in New York. If I don't have a reason to go to New York, I often plan one just to touch base. Although I do have a consulting business that is directly involved with the work I did with them, I have stayed in touch without that connection because my former colleagues are as much my friends now as they ever were. We spend a lot of our time discussing the industry and how it's changed, catching up on each other's families, and trading information about what

other former team members are doing. Like any friendship, if you invest your time in the relationship, you will both benefit.

In addition to former colleagues, it would be helpful to develop new contacts related to the industry you were in or the one you may want to enter. Getting involved in women's networking groups and specific industry networking groups are good ways to form new relationships. Don't worry about what to say when they ask you where you are working; tell them what you did in the past and that you would like to return to that industry, or use your background as a starting point to get involved in another industry.

NOTE TO FILE: 

- Remember, people like you. They will want to hear from you.
- Institutionalize your plan to keep in touch. Every month, plan to contact someone. Put it on your calendar.

Consult, Contract Out, Work Part-Time. Although working part-time from home or at a company doesn't qualify as leaving the workplace, it will allow you to be able to transition more easily to full-time work when you want to. Many women work for one client, often their previous employer, or sometimes a few, when they take on projects from home. If you can score an arrangement like that you'll have the advantage of not having to look for new customers when you're ready to take on more work. My advisory business clients came from work contacts and former clients, friends and, in one case, a soccer dad whose daughter played ball with mine. I had weeks when I didn't put in any hours and some when I would work 20 hours. Even if you average only two hours a week, you are keeping current on your business and continuing to develop your network. Doing a small amount of consulting is worthwhile just to force yourself to continue to connect with former colleagues.

If you transition to part-time work for your employer, as time goes on you may be able to ask for more flexibility such as working partially from home. Or you could swap back and forth between part-time and contract work, depending on your needs. Martha Sayre, SVP at Sotheby's auction house, had developed a niche expertise before she left her full-time position at the company. She began working on individual projects from home and eventually was able to develop her own schedule because her managers realized how difficult she would be to replace. She would decide how much she would be willing to work each month, sometimes working on a part-time schedule from her company's offices and other times doing contract work from home.

Whether you work part-time at a company's site or do contract work from home, you will be viewed by recruiters as a professional who is current with her skills, the market, and the industry. You may have been in career hibernation, but you will be infinitely more employable than if you stopped work altogether.

Doing part-time or contract work from home also allows you to avoid the challenge of trying to go back part-time after you have taken a break. Companies are much more likely to transition internal candidates than hire new ones to part-time positions.

Keep Current. Liz Lynch left Morgan Stanley when her children were in high school. She took a year off before she started consulting on her own and eventually joining her current firm. Liz said one of the most important things she did during that year was to keep current on industry news. She read about developments in her field so she would have more to offer when connecting with former colleagues. Reading also helped her start back to work again without facing a big learning curve.

Other women I spoke with agreed. You need to know what's going on in your business and have a view about the changes. You also need to acquire basic skills in new technology so you can function without too much difficulty when you re-join. Will Word and Excel still be the programs of choice in ten years in your field? Stay knowledgeable in your industry so you will know if there have been changes that will require you to update your skills.

High-Level Volunteering Can Lead to Job Offers

Susan Hill was going through a divorce and needed to return to work. Other than helping her husband with administrative aspects of his business, she hadn't worked for over 10 years. Susan had been involved in her community, though, and sat on the strategic planning board for her children's school district in northern California. Knowing she might need references when she applied for jobs, Susan asked a board member if she could offer up his name. He told her that he didn't know she was looking and asked if she would be interested in a spot at his company. She interviewed for the position, was offered a job, and now runs strategic planning for government programs at Health Net, Inc. Although her background was in finance, Susan's involvement in high-level strategic planning for the district made it possible for her to switch fields when she applied for the job.

A few of the women and a stay-at-home father I interviewed had also received job opportunities because of their high-level participation in volunteer roles. But some of them didn't immediately recognize the value they had created by leading not-for-profits or community projects. Gail, a stay-at-home mother who works with formerly drug-addicted women, said that her volunteer work was a chance to use her professional outplacement skills, such as resume writing, market research, and interviewing skills, with a very different demographic. She's now a board member for the organization, chair of the program committee, and head of the now 18-member volunteer mentor program. Yet when I asked her what she had done to stay involved in the outplacement industry, she responded, "I've been relatively dismal at that." High-level volunteering is helpful to re-enter the workforce but only if you realize that you have accomplished a lot while helping your community. You should put your achievements on your resume just as you would when describing a job, including figures and improvements. Talk about your role in increasing donations, reducing costs, or expanding membership in concrete numbers.

Child-Rearing Skills. Although we don't always recognize it, as mothers we have developed important leadership skills. We have learned a tremendous amount about how to persuade our children to follow our directions and have operated in one of the most difficult time-management environments. Even if you can't include your parenting skills on your resume, at least realize that you have developed abilities that will be immensely useful at your new job.

Overall, whether you decide to continue working, take a temporary break, or stay home full-time to care for your family and contribute to your community, I wish you luck and success. Structure your career now so that no matter what choice you make, you will be proud of your achievements. No one can take that success away from you, whether you return to work or not.

Chapter 12: Conclusion

> *Stop worrying so much. Stop being scared of the unknown. Raise the bar higher. Hug with two arms. Go find your joy. Dance a little bit before you step out into the world, because it changes the way you walk.*
>
> —Sandra Bullock, in an address to graduating high school seniors

Sandra Bullock, a surprise graduation speaker for a lucky group of high school seniors, shaped her speech around advice that she gives her son Louis. "Dance a little bit before you step out into the world, because it changes the way you walk" was one of her suggestions. Although her advice began as a life lesson for a four-year-old, it's a poignant message for career professionals. She's telling us that attitude is everything. If you go into your career, your job, or just your day with the right frame of mind, you will be happier and more confident. And those qualities are the backbone of success.

I wrote this book to give you other tips for success, some offered directly and some delivered in a way to help you figure out future solutions. When I was considering attending business school, an MBA told me something I didn't understand at the time. He said business school **teaches you how to think.** It wasn't until I enrolled and discussed case studies that I understood the meaning of his words. At business school we analyzed every possible outcome of each case and made decisions based on our own judgment, but also the input we heard from others. Most of the time, the professors never told us the right answer, which completely frustrated me. At the time I didn't understand why they didn't provide solutions, but later I realized that the answer was not important. It was gaining experience analyzing the problem that mattered. The instructors wanted to **teach us how to think.** Though you may not have an MBA, by now you should realize that analyzing each important career move relies on gathering information and advice and making your own decisions. And putting yourself in the mind of the other person, whether it's a manager or an interviewer, is one of the most useful skills you can adopt.

Success for All Stages

You may have been surprised to learn that how you present yourself will have more bearing on your success as a leader than any other factor. Above all else, colleagues need to respect you and want to work with you. These executive presence qualities are important at the first stages in your career as well, but early on, your manager will primarily focus on your attention to detail, work ethic, and teamwork. An SVP at a paper products manufacturer told me that without a doubt she progressed quickly in her organization because she was willing to do anything. Now, as a senior executive, she's acutely aware when others feel their work is beneath them. "I asked an AVP to sift through a few boxes and determine which files we should save and which we should throw out," she said. "Word got back to me that she thought I should have asked a more junior group member 'to sort through the trash.' I wanted the AVP to look at the files because she had the experience to know which of them were important. But now I no longer view her as a team player, willing to do whatever is asked of her."

I hope you've learned that throughout your career you should **exploit the unique abilities that you have.** You began your career with some inherent skills and gained others through experience; each of these make you valuable in particular areas. Become aware of the talents you have that set you apart from others and uncover ways to demonstrate those skills. Highlight them in job interviews or ask for projects that will make use of them. Volunteer to solve your manager's or your company's problems by using your talents, and you will have the double benefit of being regarded as a problem solver and a highly skilled employee. Plan your career early on to make use of your talents and organize your path to gain additional valuable skills. And remember that line experience is the key to high-level advancement in most corporate environments.

Women's Unique Path

You know that as a woman professional you aren't working on a level playing field. Gender bias is subtle though pervasive. It's fair to ask the question to yourself: **What would a man do?** But a woman's role in the office is a complicated one, and following the lead of men isn't always the right path. Go ahead and ask the question, but realize that to achieve what a man might in the same situation, you may have to act differently. Men and women become uncomfortable when women don't act according to their interpretation of how women should act. So ask for the raise, but take care in the way you ask for it to ensure you achieve your goal. A man may achieve victories at work without trying because he's measured with a different yardstick. And, while you temper the right actions with the right gender-acceptable approaches, you have to maintain your authenticity. Women have a tough menu of requirements to fulfill to get what they deserve without offending others at the same time.

We also need to juggle a few more things than men, although progressive males and corporations are slowly making improvements on that score. The number of women who have reported that they were very concerned about work/life balance has decreased from 53% to 39% over a recent two-year period.[1] Yet women still have to plan ahead so that the integration of their work and home life allows them to be successful at both. If you focus on building an arsenal of skills early in your career and become valuable within your company, you will gain the holy grail of working mothers: schedule control and flexibility. Maintaining a professional network during your breaks from work and keeping involved through part-time, contract, or consulting work will allow you greater opportunities if you return to full-time work. It's OK if you go into **career hibernation;** you can revive your career and push ahead to advance at your organization when the time is right for you.

In some ways your path is easier than women before you, but in other ways it's much harder. Your grandmothers and their mothers before them may not have had to make the choices you will be faced with because work was often something they did only until they got married. You, on the other hand, will have many tough career decisions and difficult work/life integration decisions. But that's OK, you'll know how to tackle them. **You've learned how to think.**

Acknowledgments

Many thanks to my entire team at Peterson's, including Robyn Thurman and Bernadette Webster, who made the process from Introduction to Conclusion a relatively seamless journey. I am especially grateful to my editor, Marie Galastro, who guided me with her extensive knowledge of publishing and keen-eyed editing skills.

When I first conceived of *Learn, Work, Lead*, I drafted a manuscript that became the conceptual forerunner to the current book. I thank my readers at The University of Virginia and The Amos Tuck School of Business at Dartmouth for giving me effective market feedback and inspiring me to continue to pursue the project. I'm also grateful to the many friends who read the draft and gave me valuable input, including Joy Bronson, Maureen Donahue, Gail and Peter Fritzinger, Elizabeth and Kathryn Hansen, Tom O'Conner, Annette Himes, Brenda Uyak, and Katie Uyak.

Of course the book would not have relevance without the quotes and war stories contributed by the professionals and leaders whom I am lucky enough to call my friends. Thank you Elyse Allan, Photo Anagnostoupolos, Chip Barnes, Regina Chien, Carol Fishman Cohen, Joanne Conroy, Jill Ker Conway, Melanie Czarra, John Creasy, Pat Donahue, Susan Hill, Wes Jones, Renée LaBran,

Beatrice Liu, Alyssa Lovegrove, Liz Lynch, Melinda Twomey, Vicki Neilson, Kathy McCartney, Mary Theresa McFadden, Mary McLaughlin, Sherri O'Berg, Diane Paddison, Janet Piller, John Reichenbach, Aileen Richards, Margot Rogers, Martha Sayre, KK Streator, Jennifer Urdan, David Walker, Jim Weber, and Sam Zell. I am also thankful to my colleagues at Warburg Paribas Becker, Thomson McKinnon Securities, General Foods, Prudential Insurance, Mabon Securities, and Merrill Lynch for the many rich work experiences we had together that helped me add color to these pages. The good people at Smith College and The Amos Tuck School were also especially helpful in providing resources for me to complete my writing. And thank you Sookie Lee for forever being a champion of my book project.

Along the way I received excellent advice from subject experts and business leaders who helped me form the themes in the book. I'm grateful to Linda Babcock, Frank Costanzo, Cynthia Cross, Joe Donovan, Michelle Ehrenreich, Herb Greenberg, Kim Howland, Jill Peterson, Paul Rodgers, Tina Rowlett, Helen Smith, Tom Schoenfelder, Ted Sotir, Kathy Sweeney, Mark Tierney, and Xinyun Zhu. And thank you to back cover photographer Eric Laurits for his magic with the camera.

The Muse was my training ground as its editors worked through my initial efforts to transition from banker to author. Thank you Erin Greenawald, Adrian Granzella Larssen, and, especially, Kathryn Minshew; you have provided an excellent resource for men and women seeking information about careers and a platform for me as I developed my voice as a writer. I am honored that Kathryn has written the Foreword for this book as she is a spectacular example of leadership, drive, intelligence, and poise for all young women hoping to excel in their careers.

A special thanks to Kenwyn and Andy Kindfuller who were tireless readers, editors, advisors, and cheerleaders for *Learn, Work, Lead.* Each one's intelligence, perspective, and guidance helped me shape the original drafts to the book it ultimately became.

And lastly, I thank my family, who were both inspiration for the book and key advisors in my effort. Devon was a savvy editor and my target market consultant, while Hunter provided creative input on the structure and cover of the book. Jack solved my technical problems the many times I was in need. And my husband, Jon, a successful business leader and thoughtful manager, provided valuable input during my drafting process and upon the completion of the first draft. His astute observations added significantly to the quality of the final product. I am tremendously grateful to my children and husband for not only supplying their own unique advice but also lending the critical support and encouragement that allowed me to turn my concept into reality.

Appendix: Resume Action Verbs

Action verbs give your resume power and direction. Below you will find a list of action verbs to use in your resume and cover letters.

Communication/People Skills

addressed
advertised
arbitrated
arranged
articulated
authored
clarified
collaborated
communicated
composed
condensed
conferred
consulted
contacted
conveyed
convinced
corresponded
debated
defined
developed
directed
discussed
drafted
edited
elicited
enlisted
explained
expressed
formulated
furnished
incorporated
influenced
interacted
interpreted
interviewed
involved
joined
judged
lectured
listened
marketed
mediated
moderated
negotiated
observed
outlined
participated
persuaded
presented
promoted
proposed
publicized
reconciled
recruited
referred
reinforced
reported

Reprinted with Permission from Barnard College's Career Development Office. www.barnard.edu/cd

resolved	spoke	synthesized
responded	suggested	translated
solicited	summarized	wrote
specified		

Creative Skills

acted	displayed	invented
adapted	drew	modeled
began	entertained	modified
combined	established	originated
composed	fashioned	performed
conceptualized	formulated	photographed
condensed	founded	planned
created	illustrated	revised
customized	initiated	revitalized
designed	instituted	shaped
developed	integrated	solved
directed	introduced	

Data/Financial Skills

administered	computed	netted
adjusted	conserved	planned
allocated	corrected	prepared
analyzed	determined	programmed
appraised	developed	projected
assessed	estimated	qualified
audited	forecasted	reconciled
balanced	managed	reduced
budgeted	marketed	researched
calculated	measured	retrieved

Helping Skills

adapted	coached	encouraged
advocated	collaborated	ensured
aided	contributed	expedited
answered	cooperated	facilitated
arranged	counseled	familiarized
assessed	demonstrated	furthered
assisted	diagnosed	guided
clarified	educated	helped

Reprinted with Permission from Barnard College's Career Development Office. www.barnard.edu/cd

insured
intervened
motivated
prevented
provided
referred
rehabilitated
represented
resolved
simplified
supplied
supported
volunteered

Management/Leadership Skills

administered
analyzed
appointed
approved
assigned
attained
authorized
chaired
considered
consolidated
contracted
controlled
converted
coordinated
decided
delegated
developed
directed
eliminated
emphasized
enforced
enhanced
established
executed
generated
handled
headed
hired
hosted
improved
incorporated
increased
initiated
inspected
instituted
led
managed
merged
motivated
navigated
organized
originated
overhauled
oversaw
planned
presided
prioritized
produced
recommended
reorganized
replaced
restored
reviewed
scheduled
secured
selected
streamlined
strengthened
supervised
terminated

Organizational Skills

approved
arranged
catalogued
categorized
charted
classified
coded
collected
compiled
corrected
corresponded
distributed
executed
filed
generated
incorporated
inspected
logged
maintained
monitored
obtained
operated
ordered
organized
prepared
processed
provided
purchased
recorded
registered
reserved
responded
reviewed
routed
scheduled
screened

Reprinted with Permission from Barnard College's Career Development Office.
www.barnard.edu/cd

submitted
supplied
standardized
systematized
updated
validated
verified

Research Skills

analyzed
clarified
collected
compared
conducted
critiqued
detected
determined
diagnosed
evaluated
examined
experimented
explored
extracted
formulated
gathered
inspected
interviewed
invented
investigated
located
measured
organized
researched
reviewed
searched
solved
summarized
surveyed
systematized
tested

Teaching Skills

adapted
advised
clarified
coached
communicated
conducted
coordinated
critiqued
developed
enabled
encouraged
evaluated
explained
facilitated
focused
guided
individualized
informed
instilled
instructed
motivated
persuaded
simulated
stimulated
taught
tested
trained
transmitted
tutored

Technical Skills

adapted
applied
assembled
built
calculated
computed
conserved
constructed
converted
debugged
designed
determined
developed
engineered
fabricated
fortified
installed
maintained
operated
overhauled
printed
programmed
rectified
regulated
remodeled
repaired
replaced
restored
solved
specialized
standardized
studied
upgraded
utilized

Reprinted with Permission from Barnard College's Career Development Office. www.barnard.edu/cd

Endnotes

Chapter 1

[1] E.T. Amanatullah & M. W. Morris. Negotiating gender roles: gender differences in assertive negotiating are mediated by women's fear of backlash and attenuated when negotiating on behalf of others. *Journal of Personality and Social Psychology* 2010 Feb; 98(2):256-67. doi: 10.1037/a0017094. http://www.ncbi.nlm.nih.gov/pubmed/20085399

[2] Charlotte A. Morris, M.A. The Effects of Gender on Communication in the Legal Profession. June 2009. http://wip.ncbar.org/media/2754960/effectsofgenderoncommunication.pdf

[3] http://leanin.org/book

[4] http://www.wallstreetoasis.com

Chapter 2

[1] http://www.barbarapachtersblog.com

[2] http://corporette.com

[3] http://www.corporatefashionista.com

[4] N. L. Etcoff, S. Stock, L. E. Haley, S. A. Vickery, D. M. House. Cosmetics as a Feature of the Extended Human Phenotype: Modulation of the Perception of Biologically Important Facial Signals. *PLoS ONE* 6(10): e25656, 2011. doi:10.1371/journal.pone.0025656. http://www.plosone.org/article/info%3Adoi%2F10.1371%2Fjournal.pone.0025656

[5] http://www.levo.com/officehours/warren-buffett

[6] http://www.barbarapachtersblog.com

[7] http://www.emilypost.com

[8] http://www.careerbuilder.com/share/aboutus/pressreleasesdetail.aspx?sd=2/13/2013&siteid=cbpr&sc_cmp1=cb_pr40_&id=pr40&ed=12/31/2013

[9] http://www.langerresearch.com/uploads/1130a2WorkplaceHarassment.pdf

Chapter 3

[1] http://www.forbes.com/sites/russprince/2012/03/16/what-is-a-thought-leader

[2] https://www.sec.gov/edgar/searchedgar/companysearch.html

[3] http://www.womeninecon.wsj.com/special-report.pdf

[4] http://www.sylviaannhewlett.com/find-a-sponsor.html

[5] http://www.forbes.com/sites/ciocentral/2011/12/05/the-path-to-becoming-a-fortune-500-ceo

[6] http://www.heidrick.com

[7] http://www.catalyst.org/knowledge/women-boards

Chapter 4

[1] Deborah Ward. The Familiarity Principle of Attraction: Why We're Attracted to the Wrong People and How to Attract the Right People, *Sense and Sensitivity*, *Psychology Today*, February 10, 2013. http://www.psychologytoday.com/blog/sense-and-sensitivity/201302/the-familiarity-principle-attraction

[2] http://www.theskimm.com

[3] Workplace Loyalties Change, But the Value of Mentoring Doesn't. *Knowledge@Wharton*, May 16, 2007. http://knowledge.wharton.upenn.edu/article/workplace-loyalties-change-but-the-value-of-mentoring-doesnt/#

[4] Nicole Williams. Infographic: Women and Mentoring in the U.S., *LinkedIn Official Blog*, October 25, 2011. http://blog.linkedin.com/2011/10/25/mentoring-women

[5] http://www.talentinnovation.org

[6] Sylvia Ann Hewlett. Strategic Alliances Can Make or Break Female Leaders, *HBR Blog Network, Harvard Business Review*, June 20, 2012. http://blogs.hbr.org/2012/06/strategic-alliances-can-make-o

Chapter 5

[1] Jena McGregor. Study Finds that Basically Every Single Person Hates Performance Reviews, *The Washington Post Blogs On Leadership*, January 27, 2014. http://www.washingtonpost.com/blogs/on-leadership/wp/2014/01/27/study-finds-that-basically-every-single-person-hates-performance-reviews

[2] https://www.linkedin.com/today/post/article/20140206114808-15893932-how-adobe-got-rid-of-traditional-performance-reviews

Chapter 6

[1] Robert M. Sapolsky. *Why Zebras Don't Get Ulcers*. New York: Holt Paperbacks, August 26, 2004.

[2] http://www.forbes.com/global2000/list

[3] Jack Zenger. Does Leadership Development Really Work? *Forbes.com*, May 2, 2012. http://www.forbes.com/sites/jackzenger/2012/05/02/does-leadership-development-really-work-2

[4] http://www.catalyst.org/knowledge/statistical-overview-women-workplace

[5] http://gnosis.org/Evans-Jung-Interview/evans1.html

[6] Adam M. Grant, Francesca Gino, David A. Hofmann. Reversing the extraverted leadership advantage: The role of employee productivity. *Academic Management Journal* 54:3:528–550, June 1, 2011. doi: 10.5465/AMJ.2011.61968043. http://amj.aom.org/content/54/3/528.short http://knowledge.wharton.upenn.edu/article/analyzing-effective-leaders-why-extraverts-are-not-always-the-most-successful-bosses

[7] http://www.forbes.com/profile/sam-zell

[8] J. Hall, R. C. M. Philip, K. Marwick, H. C. Whalley, L. Romaniuk, et al. Social Cognition, the Male Brain and the Autism Spectrum. *PLoS ONE* 7(12): e49033, 2012. doi:10.1371/journal.pone.0049033. http://www.plosone.org/article/info%3Adoi%2F10.1371%2Fjournal.pone.0049033

[9] Daniel Akst. If You Want a Favor Done, Ask a Woman, *Week In Ideas: Daniel Akst, The Wall Street Journal,* January 11, 2013. http://online.wsj.com/news/articles/SB10001424127887323442804578233611764440012

[10] http://www.zfco.com/media/articles/ZFCo.WP.WomenBetterThanMen.033012.pdf

[11] Chris Coddington. Qualities that Distinguish Women Leaders, *Caliper,* May 21, 2013. https://www.calipercorp.com/?s=the+qualities+that+distinguish+women+leaders

Chapter 7

[1] Linda Babcock & Sara Laschever. *Ask For It: How Women Can Use the Power of Negotiation to Get What They Really Want.* New York: Bantam Dell, 2008.

[2] Deepak Malhotra & Max Bazerman. *Negotiation Genius: How to Overcome Obstacles and Achieve Brilliant Results at the Bargaining Table and Beyond.* New York: Random House, 2007.

[3] http://www.pay-equity.org/index.html

[4] http://online.wsj.com/public/page/women-04112011.html

Chapter 8

[1] Zhaoli Song; Wendong Li; Richard D. Arvey. Associations between dopamine and serotonin genes and job satisfaction: Preliminary evidence from the ADD Health Study. *Journal of Applied Psychology*, Vol. 96(6), Nov. 2011, 1223–33. doi: 10.1037/a0024577. http://psycnet.apa.org/psycinfo/2011-15043-001

[2] http://www.bls.gov/news.release/archives/jolts_03112014.htm

Chapter 9

[1] http://www.wiu.edu/advising/docs/Holland_Code.pdf

[2] https://www.cpp.com/products/strong/index.aspx

[3] http://www.kuderjourney.com

[4] http://www.careerkey.org/career-tests/take-career-test-career-assessment.html#.U7WKh7EuK5J

[5] https://www.themuse.com/advice/the-most-fun-way-to-discover-your-passion-today

[6] Katty Kay & Claire Shipman. The Confidence Gap, *The Atlantic*, April 14, 2014. http://www.theatlantic.com/features/archive/2014/04/the-confidence-gap/359815

[7] Dr. John Sullivan. 10 Compelling Numbers That Reveal the Power of Employee Referrals, ERE.net, May 7, 2012. http://www.ere.net/2012/05/07/10-compelling-numbers-that-reveal-the-power-of-employee-referrals

[8] Lars Backstrom, Paolo Boldi, Marco Rosa, Johan Ugander, & Sebastiano Vigna. "Four Degrees of Separation," November 19, 2011. arXiv:1111.4570 [cs.SI]. http://arxiv.org/abs/1111.4570 (Article on study can be found at: http://www.bbc.co.uk/news/technology-15844230)

[9] https://www.linkedin.com/static?key=what_is_linkedin

[10] http://www.womenintechnology.org

[11] https://www.ellevatenetwork.com

[12] http://www.levo.com/connections

[13] http://leanin.org/circles

[14] Real-Time Insight Into the Market for Entry-Level STEM Jobs, *Burning Glass Careers in Focus,* 2014. http://www.burning-glass.com/research/stem

[15] http://www.glassdoor.com/index.htm

[16] http://www.indeed.com

[17] http://money.msn.com

[18] http://finance.yahoo.com

Chapter 10

[1] Sarah Chang. The Little Interview Mistakes—That Cost You Big Time. Career Advice, The Muse, March 25, 2014. https://www.themuse.com/advice/the-little-interview-mistakesthat-cost-you-big-time

Chapter 11

[1] PwC's NextGen: A Global Generational Study 2013: Evolving Talent Strategy to Match the New Workforce Reality. http://www.pwc.com/en_GX/gx/hr-management-services/pdf/pwc-nextgen-study-2013.pdf

[2] http://www.heidrick.com/Search-Results?SearchString=advanced+degrees

[3] Sylvia Ann Hewlett & Melinda Marshall. Does Female Ambition Require Sacrifice? HBR Blog Network, *Harvard Business Review,* February 25, 2011. http://blogs.hbr.org/2011/02/does-female-ambition-require-a

[4] Kathy Caprino. Busting the Myth That Women Aren't As Ambitious As Men, *Forbes*, November 28, 2011. http://www.forbes.com/sites/kathycaprino/2011/11/28/busting-the-myth-that-women-arent-as-ambitious-as-men

[5] http://alphanow.thomsonreuters.com/ebooks/women-in-the-workplace/#13

[6] http://www.wmmsurveys.com/WhatMomsChoose.pdf

Chapter 12

[1] The Career Peak Paradox: New Citi/LinkedIn Survey Suggests Professionals Believe Success is a Moving Target, June 4, 2014. http://www.businesswire.com/news/home/20140604005166/en/Career-Peak-Paradox-CitiLinkedIn-Survey-Suggests-Professionals#.U7sEGrEuK5K

Index